Illustrated

MOPAR
BUYER'S GUIDE™

Evolution from classics to muscle cars 1941-74
Chrysler, Dodge, Plymouth,
Imperial and DeSoto

Peter C. Sessler

Motorbooks International
Publishers & Wholesalers Inc.
Osceola, Wisconsin 54020, USA ®

First published in 1989 by Motorbooks
International Publishers & Wholesalers Inc, P O
Box 2, 729 Prospect Avenue, Osceola, WI 54020
USA

Printed and bound in the United States of
America

Library of Congress Cataloging-in-Publication Data

Sessler, Peter C.
    Illustrated Mopar buyer's guide.

    1. Chrysler automobile—Purchasing.   I. Title.
TL215.C55S47   1989   629.2'222   88-13732
ISBN 0-87938-332-1 (soft)

On the front cover: The 1969 Dodge Charger
Daytona and 1970 Plymouth AAR 'Cuda owned
by Gary and Cindy Moe. *Michael Dregni*

On the back cover: Jerry Rushing's infamous 300D,
Traveller, the moonshine-running muscle car.

I thank all those who contributed to this
book with photos and information, with
special thanks to Richard Dangler, Wayne
Hartye, Alan Linsky, Guy Morice, Alan
Ralston, Don Rook, Don Snyder, Walt Van
Deppen, Ron Wenger and Chrysler Corporation.

Contents

Introduction

The image that comes to mind for a lot of people when the subject of Chrysler automobiles is brought up, is one of big rumbling muscle cars. I think in this book you will discover that Chrysler automobiles have more depth and scope to offer than this stereotypical image would convey. Chrysler has also built some of the most fabulously unique cars, cars with incredible styling and performance.

Chrysler, along with the rest of the auto industry, was in a strong position after World War II. They sold all the cars that could be built to a car-starved public even though styling was about as conservative as you could get. After 1949, the public showed a preference for the sleeker offerings from Ford and General Motors, to the point that Chrysler fell to third place behind Ford in 1952. The situation worsened by 1954, but the Virgil Exner–styled cars of 1955 reversed Chrysler's fortunes, and by 1957 Chrysler clearly took the lead from General Motors as the industry's styling leader.

The stunning 1957 Chrysler line-up shook the industry. Unfortunately, Chrysler was unable to follow it up: as Lee Iacocca has said, it's styling that sells cars but it's value that keeps customers coming back. It really was a Catch-22 situation because practical cars did not sell unless they were also attractive. The fifties and sixties were especially style-sensitive eras. It became important not to be seen driving the previous year's model.

By the early sixties Chrysler's styling had run amok. What had originally been clean, elegant and innovative was taken to such extremes that the cars no longer appealed to the American public. During the rest of the decade Chrysler played catch-up ball, following rather than leading in terms of styling. They did, however, produce one of the sixties' most visually exciting automobiles, the 1968 Dodge Charger.

The relative prosperity of the sixties gave way to the trauma of the seventies—two oil scares and a brush with bankruptcy—but Chrysler again showed resiliency and bounced back, to produce the eighties' most innovative cars, the Voyager and Caravan minivans.

Chrysler has always been associated with performance, and this has not necessarily been in keeping with Chrysler's conservative image. It seems as though there has always been a fringe group within the company which managed to get by management some pretty interesting automobiles and engineering features. The most well known examples are the Hemi engines and the wild Daytona and Super Bird.

Chryslers are just starting to get the recognition they so richly deserve. I have tried to include all the major collectibles produced since 1945. The Town & Country series is an obvious stand-out as they are the best of all the wooden-bodied cars produced in the forties. The Chrysler 300 Letter Series, combining luxury and performance, are starting to skyrocket in value. As unique, but mostly unknown, are the DeSoto Adventurers. The Plymouth Fury was at one time the division's premier offering. The Imperial, which never really caught on, showed that Chrysler knew how to build a luxury automobile.

When it came to the muscle car era, the Hemi ruled. Hemi-powered Dodges and Plymouths are still hot today; they are indeed the ultimate expression of sixties performance.

Obviously, originality is important here. If you are new to the hobby, you'll find that there are many levels of originality, and much depends on how you are going to use the car. If you are intending to show the car, be forewarned. A car is considered to be original only if it has been restored to factory specifications. It has to be exactly in the same condition as when it left the factory, using the same type and kind of parts that the car originally came with. Dealer-installed equipment is a vast gray area, constantly debated, as is owner-installed equipment, whether to improve performance or make the car safer. The fifties and sixties tire technology left a lot to be desired, for example. You'll find that the vast majority of enthusiasts have cars that are modified and are not "true" originals. Naturally the more original the car, the greater its worth.

My own personal view is that a car can be modified and not reduce its inherent value, provided it can be returned to original condition. This means that if you are going to install headers or an electronic ignition system, keep the factory stock parts so that if you do decide to sell it you can easily return it to stock.

Simple modifications can also be used to update these cars and make them that much more enjoyable. A great deal of the enjoyment that can be derived from owning a collectible Chrysler is from driving one. The muscle cars, in particular, may be crude when compared to the computerized techno wizardry that is available today but they sure get your heart beating faster. They were, and still are, fun to drive.

As far as restoring a Chrysler, you'll find that there are many sources for engine and drivetrain components, and parts are available. The difficulty in restoring Chryslers is finding interior pieces: trim, upholstery, body parts and so on. Unlike other collectibles which you can practically rebuild by just calling a toll-free number and charging all the parts you need to your credit card, you'll have to do quite a bit of legwork if you are trying to restore a Chrysler. There is no large reproduction industry serving the Mopar enthusiast because most of the desirable cars were built in small numbers. In my research, I found that there are many rare cars out there rotting away simply because there aren't any parts available to restore them.

For this reason, it is important that you try to find a car that requires the least amount of work. It may be tempting to buy a basket case, but without question, you'll find that you'll underestimate the final cost of the restoration. Your best bet is to join some of the clubs listed in the Appendix, look at the want ads in the club magazines and subscribe to *Hemmings Motor News*. You'll find that the asking prices in *Hemmings* can be all over the place for similar cars. Under the parts headings, however, you'll get a fairly good idea of what parts cost and what their availability is.

You'll note that I haven't included a price guide in this book; by the time it is published, it will be out of date. You can refer to the *Old Cars Price Guide*, which is published several times a year, or *Hemmings*. But don't treat them as bibles; they are just an indication. By the same token, rare cars will rarely be advertised, but I guarantee you that if the owner belongs to a club, someone in the club will know about the car. Parts dealers who specialize in Mopars are also knowledgeable about who has what for sale.

My goal in writing this book has been to present the most desirable Mopars from 1945 on. I hope the information and photos which follow will enable you to recognize and appreciate the best that Chrysler has to offer.

Investment rating

★★★★★ These are the most sought after and also the rarest Mopars. They are already expensive and have the best potential for continued appreciation.

★★★★ Still rare and sought after, cars in this category were built in greater numbers than those rating five stars, but still are a solid investment.

★★★ Built in still greater numbers, these Mopars are more readily available and thus less expensive to acquire. This category also includes Mopars built in limited quantities but which have not yet caught on.

★★ These Mopars haven't caught on because they were built in great numbers and show no uniqueness. Relatively inexpensive to acquire, they may be expensive to restore so be careful here.

★ This category includes any radically modified car, any race car and any car with the wrong engine.

★★★★	**1941-42 Town & Country**
★★★★★	**1946-49 Town & Country convertible**
★★★★	**1946-50 Town & Country sedans**

1941-50 Chrysler Town & Country

The Town & Country name has magic. Ask anyone, and they'll tell you it's a Chrysler convertible from the 1940s with wood on the sides. That's the image the name conveys, even though hardtops, sedans and wagons were built as well. These were big and luxurious, the most expensive Chryslers (except for the Crown Imperials) available in the late 1940s.

1941-42

The name Town & Country first appeared in March 1941, and only on station wagons. They were built in either six- or nine-

The first Town & Country was this 1941 station wagon. This is the nine-passenger version. *Chrysler Corporation*

The 1942 wagon got a slight restyle, with a new grille, bumper and fenders. Spotlight, white plastic trim rings and roof rack were options. *Applegate & Applegate*

This factory photo shows a 1946 Town & Country convertible. Convertibles were more popular than the sedans. *Applegate & Applegate*

passenger configurations on the 121.5 inch Windsor chassis, powered by a 112 hp six-cylinder engine.

The station wagon was also available during the abbreviated 1942 model run, again in the same six- and nine-passenger configurations. During both 1941 and 1942, one nine-passenger prototype using the 127.5 inch New Yorker platform and eight-cylinder engine was built. Compared to what was available at the time, the Town & Country wagon stood out with its curvy, streamlined styling, while competing makes looked utilitarian and trucklike.

The wooden bodies were seasoned white ash, while the inner panels were Honduran mahogany plywood, treated with three coats of varnish. A Chrysler brochure stated "The Chrysler Town and Country car is designed and built for those who recognize and appreciate fine things. It has the grace and elegance of a yacht. In fact, the wood is quite similar to the planking of a ship, both in construction and treatment. Care of the finish should be thought of in terms of boating, rather than motoring." In fact, Chrysler recommended that the wood surfaces be stripped and revarnished each year in order to maintain their gloss.

Pekin Wood Products Company of West Helena, Arkansas, which was owned by Chrysler, made the wooden body parts. From there, the parts and sometimes subassemblies were shipped to the Jefferson Avenue Chrysler plant in Detroit, where the finished bodies were mounted on their chassis. With so much handwork involved, the Town & Country was not inexpensive to produce, yet post-World War II production took off.

1946–48

The bulk of Town & Country production occurred during the period from 1946 to

Only seven two-door hardtop coupes were built in 1946. *Applegate & Applegate*

A 1947 Town & Country came with white side-wall tires. Woodwork is difficult to restore. *Robert Jochim*

1948. No wagons were offered, just a convertible built on the 127.5 inch chassis and powered by the 135 hp L-head eight-cylinder engine and a six-cylinder four-door sedan

built on the 121.5 inch chassis. A two-door brougham, a two-door convertible built on the shorter chassis and seven two-door hardtops were also built in 1946. These three were listed in Chrysler brochures.

Matching the Town & Country's unique styling was its luxurious interior. The convertibles were finished in leather and Bedford cloth, while the less glamorous sedans used combinations of leather or vinyl with saran plastic or cloth. The convertibles came with matching leather and cloth door padding; the sedans featured bare wood door panels.

In 1947 Chrysler replaced the mahogany veneer inserts with Di Noc decals simulating mahogany and walnut grains as a cost-saving measure.

1949

After minor trim changes for 1948, the next restyle occurred in the 1949 Town & Country, which was available only as a convertible, although at one point Chrysler had planned a hardtop. The convertible was built

Yes, you can still find desirable, unrestored Town & Countrys hidden away in the proverbial barn, as this car is. A good $20,000 will probably be needed to restore this sedan.

on a 131.5 inch wheelbase and featured the first major restyle for Chrysler since the war ended. Many consider the 1949 to be the best looking of the lot. The 1949 used an all-steel body with the white ash framing performing only a decorative function. Di Noc decals were used on the early 1949s, while the later cars simply had the metal panels that matched the rest of the car.

Chrysler has always prided itself on being a company dedicated to engineering, and in 1949 some important additions were made. Safety-Rim wheels were designed to hold the tire in place during a blow-out. Full Flow oil filters were attached directly on the engine without connecting lines. And brake linings were bonded to the brake shoes, resulting in greater intervals between brake jobs.

1950

The year 1950 was the last for the Town & Country as a separate series. Only one model was offered, a Newport two-door hardtop with different grille and fenders.

Some attribute the Town & Country's demise in part to the high cost of repairs—for example, in 1948 a standard deck lid cost $39, while a Town & Country lid cost $273. Although this is true, few people base their

Eight-cylinder engine provided leisurely acceleration. This is in a 1949 model.

purchase of a car on repair costs, especially in the price range of the Town & Country. The reality of it all was that the woodie look had been played out, not only at Chrysler, but at all other manufacturers as well. The Town & Country name, however, continued to be used on Chrysler station wagons.

Prospects

Town & Country cars are by far the most desirable of all the woodies built in the 1940s, with the convertibles leading the way. It is not uncommon for a superb example to fetch $50,000 and more, and there is

The 1949 convertible is considered to be the best looking. This car has painted-in body panels.

A 1949 convertible interior.

no reason for prices not to continue their upward climb. Depending on a car's condition, you may still be able to find a "steal" in the $20,000 range, but be aware of the problems and the expense that you can encounter with wood: varnish buildup and dry rot—and finding someone to work on them. Still, few cars (if any) built in the 1940s can match the style, glamour, grace and presence of a Town & Country convertible.

Last of the Town & Country series was this 1950 hardtop. *Applegate & Applegate*

Chapter 2

★★★★	**1955 C300**
★★★★⌟	**1956 300B**
★★★★★	**1957 300C**
★★★★★	**1958 300D**
★★★★⌟	**1959 300E**
★★★★★	**1960 300F**
★★★★	**1961 300G**
★★★★	**1962 300H**
★★★⌟	**1963 300J**
★★★	**1964 300K**
★★★	**1965 300L**
★★★⌟	**1964-65 300K and 300L convertibles**

1955–65 Chrysler 300 Letter Series

Before we explore the fabulous Chrysler 300s, let's define exactly what the 300s were. The 300 Letter Series, as they are called, were first introduced as a 1955 model, the C300. Subsequently, the 300B came out as a 1956 model, the 300C in 1957 and so on, until in 1965 the last Letter Series, the 300L, appeared (there was no 300I). However, there are non-Letter 300s as well, beginning with the 1962 model year. Chrysler applied the 300 designation to more sedate models to improve sales. This practice continued until the 1971 model year. The last time Chrysler used the 300 name was in 1979. No

The most talked about car of 1955, the Chrysler C300. This factory photo shows the optional wire wheels. *Applegate & Applegate*

15

The C300 used the Imperial grille but retained the New Yorker bumper. This particular car has owner-installed rear sideview mirrors. *Larry Bledsoe*

You only have to look at other 1955 makes to see how elegant and simple the C300 was. Center car has the standard wheel cover, basically an Imperial unit with a checkered insert. Wire wheels came in sets of five. Center car has non-standard fog lights and all have owner-installed rear sideview mirrors. *Larry Bledsoe*

doubt Chrysler will use the 300 name again in the future.

Because of the varied use of the 300 moniker, a fair amount of controversy exists within Chrysler circles as to what constitutes a 300. Dyed-in-the-wool purists recognize only the 1955–61 models as true 300s because these lived up to the concept of an exclusive racer built for the street. The Milestone Car Society also recognized these as Milestone cars, that is, modern classics, which tends to reinforce this concept. Others feel that true 300s include all the Letter cars ending with the 300L. Still others feel that all Chrysler automobiles bearing the 300 name should be considered as true 300s.

I don't back any particular point of view, but I will say that this sort of controversy is essentially unresolvable and that it is not unique to the 300s. For example, Shelby Mustang purists feel that only the 1965–67 versions are true Shelby Mustangs because

The C300 dash. Note awkward position of shift lever. *Larry Bledsoe*

The 331 ci FirePower V-8. Triangular air cleaner and valve covers were painted gold. *Larry Bledsoe*

the later 1968–70 models were designed and built by Ford.

Certainly the early 300 Letter cars are far more valuable, yet the other 300s can provide just as much satisfaction.

1955 C300

The C300 is a car that happened to be introduced at exactly the right time. There are several reasons why Chrysler developed the C300, and at the same time, the C300 served as a focus for several elements that ensured its success and the success of the rest of the Chrysler line-up in 1955.

Certainly, engineering and utilitarian value are important factors that govern the success or failure of a particular car or car line. Chrysler products of the early 1950s stressed these factors, featuring interior size versus exterior bulk. Yet styling sold cars more than any other factor. Chrysler sales fluctuated: 1951 and 1953 were good years, but 1954 proved to be a disaster with

sales dropping over 450,000 units compared with 1953. By 1954, Chrysler styling was clearly not in favor with the public which preferred the sleeker offerings from GM and Ford.

Fortunately, the Virgil Exner-designed models of 1955 arrived just in time; Exner had been Chrysler's chief stylist since 1953. The cars were sleeker, cleaner, longer and much more attractive. The corporation dubbed the new styling as the Forward Look. The buying public showed its approval by buying more Chrysler products than ever before. The C300 incorporated the best features of the Forward Look, and as a top-of-the-line prestige model, it fit in quite nicely with the rest of the model line-up.

At the same time, an image car was needed to compete with the limited-production Chevrolet Corvette and the new Ford Thunderbird. The C300, however, was a high-performance image car, and nothing made in 1955 could touch it in terms of per-

The 1956 300B was essentially the same car, but the rear is more attractive.

formance. Performance is what has made the C300 famous, and that fame is due to Chrysler's most famous engine—the Hemi.

The first Hemi V-8, called the FirePower, was introduced in 1951 Chrysler Imperials and New Yorkers, even though it had been in development on and off since 1935. It differed from other conventional ohv designs because the combustion chamber was hemispherical, which all boiled down to greater efficiency, and that meant greater output. All things being equal, the Hemi design tended to produce horsepower at higher rpm. Low-end torque and acceleration were about the same as with a typical wedge design, yet as rpm increased, the Hemi outran the wedge. The Hemi was known for its incredible high rpm acceleration.

The year 1958 unfortunately was the last for the first-generation Chrysler Hemi but the Hemi design was used again by various Chrysler cars from 1966 to 1971. The only other domestic manufacturer to offer a production Hemi engine was Ford which used the Boss 429 engine in a limited-production 1969–70 Mustang.

Soon after the FirePower's introduction, the engine found a home in Briggs Cunningham's C-2 roadsters that competed in the famous Le Mans race in 1951. One of these cars managed to finish eighteenth. Carl Kiekhaefer, the Mercury Outboard Motor manufacturer, entered two Hemi-powered Chryslers in the 1951 Carrera PanAmericana (or Mexican Road Race). One car managed to finish sixteenth. This and other race appearances generated considerable interest in the FirePower Hemi. From 1951 to 1953, more and more racers used this engine and even an Indy version was developed, but because it outpowered the established Offenhauser engine, last minute rule changes made it uncompetitive and it did not race.

The FirePower, then, was the natural choice for the C300. Displacement was set at 331 ci as offered in other Chrysler cars, but with the use of two four-barrel Carter WCFB carburetors and a solid lifter camshaft that was close to the race 331s. Power output was 300 hp—the first American production engine with such a high output—

1955 Chrysler C300	
Engine	
Type	V-8
Bore x stroke, in.	3.81 x 3.63
Displacement, cubic in.	331
Compression ratio	8.5:1
Horsepower	300@5200 rpm
Torque	345@3200
Chassis and drivetrain	
Transmission	2-spd automatic
Front suspension	Independent, coil springs
Rear suspension	Live axle, leaf springs
Axle ratio	3.54:1
Brakes, front/rear	Drum/drum
General	
Wheelbase, in.	126
Height, in.	60.1
Width, in.	79.1
Length, in.	218.6
Weight, lb.	4,005

which earned the 300 designation for the car.

As for the car itself, for cost reasons, it was based on the New Yorker two-door hardtop with rear quarters adapted from the Windsor, and to lend prestige, the Imperial grille was used (as was the dash). Unlike other Chrysler offerings of 1955, the C300 kept body ornamentation at a minimum, to the point that no back-up lights or outside

The 1957 300C was totally restyled, looking unlike any other American car. Mean-looking grille had a definite European flavor. Outside rearview mirror was optional in 1957.

Simple rear-end treatment characterized the 300C. One easy way to tell the difference between a 300C and 300D from the rear is to look at the taillights. The 300-C's were much larger.

rearview mirrors were offered. Coupled with only a single color paint scheme limited to black, white or red, all this simplicity tended to accentuate and define the C300's sleekness, which resulted in a determined yet graceful look. The C300 really stood out—styling of the day usually dictated wild two-tone paint and lavish use of chrome which more than approached garishness.

The interior was finished in tan leather and vinyl. Options included power steering, four-way power bench seat, power windows, radio, heater, tinted glass and, at a rather expensive $617, a set of five Kelsey-Hayes wire wheels that were also used on the 1954 Imperial. Air conditioning was not available. All C300s used a beefed-up two-speed automatic transmission, the Power-Flite, with a higher stall-speed torque converter. Standard axle ratio was 3.54:1, with the option of other ratios ranging from 3.36:1 to 4.10:1. Interestingly, the standard power brakes were drums all around, and the Imperial four-wheel discs were not used on the C300. Higher-rate coil springs in front and leaves at the rear along with heavy-duty shocks enabled the C300 to corner better than any other Chrysler offering in 1955.

For its time, the C300 was a fast car. The 0-60 mph acceleration came in at about ten seconds and the quarter-mile in the high seventeens, depending on axle ratio. A top speed of 130 mph could be reached.

Appearing in January 1956 as a midyear introduction, which also coincided with the Daytona Speed Trials, the C300 was a fan-

For the first time, the 300 was available as a convertible. Note upswept rear fins and large taillight lenses. The 300s also got red, white and blue medallions on the rear fenders, interior and grille. *Chrysler Corporation*

tastic success. It set many records and also won the Daytona Grand National race. By the end of the season, the C300 had won both NASCAR and AAA stock car championships, truly a formidable achievement for a new car. Credit goes to Carl Kiekhaefer and his Mercury Outboard team.

Prospects

A total of 1,725 1955 C300s were built, and best estimates indicate that less than 200 survive today. Most that still exist are probably restored. Parts availability is poor, and if you do get a non-restored or partially restored example, make sure that you have a source for parts. The reason that the car you are looking at may not have been restored could be a lack of parts.

Prices range from $5,000 to about $18,000 for a restored C300. Expect continued and fairly quick appreciation.

It is important not to forget what the C300 was in 1956: an exclusive automobile that most of the buying public could not afford. It was a car that had luxury, performance, engineering and status, and it appealed to the same people who today buy Mercedes, BMWs and Jaguars.

1956 300B

Following the success of the C300, the next in the series was the 300B, also introduced as a midyear model, in January 1957. At a quick glance, the car seemed similar to the C300, yet it featured mechanical and styling differences.

Visually, the biggest difference was the restyled rear end, which had restrained (compared to later 300s') fins. These enhanced the sleekness and the appearance of the car. The front of the car, except for some minor detail differences, still used the Imperial grille. Notice also that an outside rearview mirror was used and that the rear taillights incorporated back-up lights.

Mechanically, by increasing the bore by 0.13 inch, cubic displacement increased to 354 on the FirePower Hemi. Compression ratio was increased to 9:1 from 8.5:1, and this resulted in 340 hp. Later in the year, a 355 hp version was made available. The extra horsepower was a result of the compression ratio having been raised to 10:1 and the use of a special three-inch exhaust system. The three-inch system was optional on the 340 hp engine.

A few 1957 300Cs were built with this type of headlight configuration. Quad headlights were not yet legal in all states, a situation which would change by 1958. *J. R. Beck*

1956 Chrysler 300B

Engine

Type	V-8
Bore x stroke, in.	3.94 x 3.63
Displacement, cubic in.	354
Compression ratio	9.0:1 (10.0:1 opt.)
Horsepower	340@5200 (355@5200 opt.)
Torque	385@3400 (405@3400 opt.)

Chassis and drivetrain

Transmission	2-spd automatic (early), 3-spd automatic (late)
Optional transmission	3-spd manual
Front suspension	Independent, coil springs
Rear suspension	Live axle, leaf springs
Axle ratio	3.54:1
Brakes, front/rear	Drum/drum

General

Wheelbase, in.	126
Height, in.	59.4
Width, in.	79.1
Length, in.	222.7
Weight, lb.	4,145

Performance

0-60 mph	8.2
¼-mile e.t.@mph	NA
Source	*Motorsport, 6/1956*

Just as important as the higher horsepower was the 300B's ability to use the power for increased performance, due to the optional three-speed manual transmission (not available with power steering and brakes). Off-the-line acceleration was greatly improved: 0–60 mph times in the low eight-second range were possible. Additional flexibility was added when the two-speed PowerFlite transmission was replaced by a cast-iron-case three-speed TorqueFlite automatic. Interestingly, Chrysler equipped only thirty-one cars with the three-speed manual. Other improvements included a twelve-volt electrical system and the availability of air conditioning.

On the track, the 300s continued to perform well with the Kiekhaefer cars doing most of the winning; this was the last season that his cars would compete because he pulled out of circle-track racing. In a sense, Kiekhaefer was too successful. There were

The 392 ci FirePower put out 375 hp in standard form. As before, air cleaners and valve covers were painted gold. *J. R. Beck*

times when his cars were booed because they usually won. His competitors constantly protested his cars, yet never proved that he cheated. Rather, Kiekhaefer was a perfectionist, and teamwork and extremely careful preparation enabled his cars to beat everyone else's, including those of factory teams. An extremely proud and independent man, by the end of 1957, Kiekhaefer had had enough and withdrew from racing.

Prospects

Total production of the 300B was 1,102. As with the C300, few remain. I have given the 300B four and a half stars—half a star more than the C300, because it is rarer and because its mechanical improvements and styling make it a better car. Current prices are about the same as for the C300, $5,000 to $18,000, and you can definitely expect sharp appreciation.

1957 300C

The year 1957 brought the third 300 in the continuing series, the 300C. Introduced to the public on December 8, 1956, it was very different from its predecessors—not only was the styling changed, but the car,

1957 Chrysler 300C	
Engine	
Type	V-8
Bore x stroke, in.	4.00 x 3.90
Displacement, cubic in.	392
Compression ratio	9.25:1 (10.0:1 opt.)
Horsepower	375@5200 (390@5400 opt.)
Torque	420@4000 (430@4200 opt.)
Chassis and drivetrain	
Transmission	3-spd automatic
Optional transmission	3-spd manual
Front suspension	Independent, torsion bars
Rear suspension	Live axle, leaf springs
Axle ratio	3.36:1
Brakes, front/rear	Drum/drum
General	
Wheelbase, in.	126
Height, in.	54.7 (55 convertible)
Width, in.	78.8
Length, in.	219.2
Weight, lb.	4,235 (4,390 convertible)
Performance	
0–60 mph	7.7
¼-mile e.t.@mph	NA
Source	*Motor Life, 5/1957*

along with the rest of the Chrysler line, featured significant engineering improvements as well.

The Flite Sweep show cars of 1955 influenced the styling, which meant fins—big, big fins. They were quite graceful and balanced, and they even looked functional. According to Chrysler, they added stability at speeds over 60–70 mph. This was Virgil Exner at his best, and the industry looked to

There were two Derham-modified 300s built. One was a 300B and the other was this 300C. Modifications included the white canvas roof and the removal of all side trim. In the interior, Stewart Warner instruments took the place of the originals. Derham, no longer in business, modified cars for the rich and famous. *Merle Wolfer*

The 1958 300D featured restyled taillights. The grille was the same. Small rectangular grille beneath headlights provided fresh air to the front brakes for improved cooling. *Ken Driedger*

Chrysler for styling leadership, at least for the next two to three years.

The 300C was still based on the New Yorker and its 126 inch wheelbase. Besides the rear fins, the front of the car became decidedly mean with its large trapezoidal grille. At that time, writer Bill Carroll coined the term "Beautiful Brute," and since then it has been used to describe all 300s.

In addition to the hardtop, a gorgeous convertible was available as well. Color choice expanded to five, with Parade Green and Copper Brown joining white, red and black. The interior was still made only in a tan leather. Special-order colors were available as well, and this was indicated by the numbers 888 on the car's data plate.

The FirePower Hemi was enlarged to 392 ci, and output increased to 375 hp. The added displacement was arrived at by boring and stroking: 4.00x3.90 inches. Increasing the stroke in any engine has the tendency to increase low-end torque at the expense of upper rpm capability, not a big factor on a

street engine and certainly not on the Fire-Power. To help the Hemi breath even better, intake valve size was increased to two inches from 1.94. The 300C was still America's most powerful production car.

Transmission choice in 1957 was limited to the push-button-controlled three-speed TorqueFlite automatic standard and a three-speed manual optional. The three-speed manual was only available with the engine-chassis performance package.

The biggest engineering change that the 300C shared with the rest of the Chrysler product line-up for 1957 was the introduction of the torsion bar front suspension called Torsion-Aire by Chrysler. The benefits of torsion bars were improved handling without a corresponding ride penalty. Torsion-Aire, coupled with other improvements such as a lower center of gravity, a wide lateral spring base and a higher roll center, made the 1957 Chryslers the best handling cars in the industry. The 300C received torsion bars that were forty per-

Traveller, looking outwardly very stock, was in reality a highly modified car. Suspension was designed to sit a normal ride height with a full load of 'shine.

If you are going to run 'shine, you might as well
do it in style. Switches operated taillights and oil
dump tank. Note hefty seat belts.

cent stiffer, providing race-car-type ride and performance.

The major options included air conditioning, power steering, six-way power seat, power windows, radio, heater, tinted glass and outside rearview mirrors. Various rear-axle ratios enabled the owner to fine-tune acceleration versus cruising capabilities. An optional exhaust system available for the hardtop utilized larger 2½ inch pipes. The convertible was limited to a two-inch system due to X-member interference.

The engine-chassis performance package included the 390 hp version of the Fire-Power. The additional 15 hp resulted from an increased compression ratio of 10.0:1 vs 9.25:1, and a hotter camshaft. The three-speed manual was available only with this package, and the lack of power steering and power brakes made the 300C so-equipped a bear to drive. Only eighteen were made.

As far as performance goes, the 300C accelerated quicker than its predecessor; yet at the Flying Mile at Daytona, it was slightly slower at 134.128 mph. Top speed depended on rear-axle ratio: 150 mph was possible. Handling was considered excellent, but it is definitely dated by today's standards. The 9.00x14 tires were awful, and the drum brakes just faded away under hard use. Still, few cars can rival its cruising capabilities and its seemingly effortless acceleration at higher speed.

Prospects

Production in 1957 increased to 1,767 hardtops and 484 convertibles. Of the two, the convertible is more desirable and usually fetches $3,000 to $5,000 more than the hardtop. As with the C300 and 300B, you can expect more than normal appreciation in the years to come, especially with the convertible.

1958 300D

The year 1957 proved so successful for Chrysler that few changes were made for

A highly modified 392 allowed *Traveller* to cruise at 140 mph.

The 1959 300E featured a restyled grille insert
and a restyled rear-end treatment. *Guy Morice*

the 1958 model year and that included the 300D. Some minor styling changes, some engine refinements, but basically it was the same car.

The D did not have the windshield visor that the C had, rear taillights were smaller and the interior had differently styled upholstery and door panels. Standard color selection grew to six with additional special-order colors available. It seems to me, however, that white must have been the most popular color because most of the cars surviving today are white. The option list grew slightly, but the basic power options continued. As with the 300C, the D's three-speed manual was available without power steering, power brakes or air conditioning. Low production does make a manual-equipped 300D rare, and that does add to its desirability. It is not a fun car to drive, though.

The 392 ci FirePower's compression ratio was raised to 10.0:1 for a 380 hp output.

Cam timing was slightly subdued, which resulted in a smoother idle. The 390 horse carbureted version was unfortunately not available.

Instead, Chrysler tried to market a Bendix EFI (electronic fuel injection) version rated at 390 hp. EFI is rather ho-hum today, yet in 1958 it was advanced—in fact, too advanced, as the system proved to be not only unreliable but also too expensive. Only sixteen cars were so equipped, and most of these were later converted to the two four-barrel carburetor setup. Chrysler has always prided itself as being, more than anything else, a company dedicated to engineering, and the EFI system was its answer to the mechanical injection system used on the 1957 Corvette, which was far more reliable.

Prospects

The 300D has one distinction that makes it not only a desirable collector car but also unique. It is the last Letter Series that came

The 300E got the swivel front seats as standard equipment. This car also has power windows.
Guy Morice

29

1958 Chrysler 300D

Engine
Type	V-8
Bore x stroke, in.	4.00 x 3.90
Displacement, cubic in.	392
Compression ratio	10.0:1 (10.0:1 opt.)
Horsepower	380@5200 (390@5200 opt.)
Torque	435@3600 (435@3600 opt.)

Chassis and drivetrain
Transmission	3-spd automatic
Optional transmission	3-spd manual
Front suspension	Independent, torsion bars
Rear suspension	Live axle, leaf springs
Axle ratio	3.31:1
Brakes, front/rear	Drum/drum

General
Wheelbase, in.	126
Height, in.	55.2 (55.6 convertible)
Width, in.	79.6
Length, in.	220.2
Weight, lb.	4,305 (4,475 convertible)

Performance
0-60 mph	8.4
¼-mile e.t.@mph	16.0@85
Source	*Road & Track*, 4/1958

with the Hemi engine. For cost reasons, later Letter Series cars were equipped with wedge-head engines. Some of these were faster, yet none have that indescribable something, the mystique of a Hemi.

The year 1958 was a bad one for the industry. Production of the 300D was 618 hardtops and only 191 convertibles. For this reason, 300D convertibles are currently somewhat more expensive than 300C convertibles.

The 1958 300D has a bit of folklore associated with it. Because Chryslers were so powerful and well built, they proved to be popular with moonshiners in the South. The most famous of these was the 300D used by Jerry Rushing. With a full load of 'shine (adding at least 2,000 pounds to the car's weight), *Traveller*, as Rushing named his 300D, could and did hit 140 mph. Naturally the big Chrysler was modified with a

The big 413 wedge replaced the Hemi. *Guy Morice*

The 1960 300F is considered among the most desirable of all 300s. Continental spare, an Exner touch, available on other Chrysler cars for several years, came with the 300F.

reworked engine and suspension, and some of its "owner-installed" modifications included a twenty-gallon oil dump tank and a switch to turn off *Traveller*'s brakelights. If a

police car got too close, a flick of another switch (straight from James Bond) would spray a fine mist of oil on the road with predictable results. Naturally, Rushing and *Traveller* were never caught.

Years later, Hollywood adapted Rushing's escapades for a TV show, called "The Dukes of Hazzard." Rather than use rare 300Ds, a Dodge Charger named *General Lee* took the place of *Traveller*. *Traveller*, by the way, was the name of General Robert E. Lee's horse.

1959 300E

The third year of the redesigned Chrysler line was 1959. Sales improved overall as the economy pulled itself out of the recession, yet sales did not grow appreciably at Chrysler. The finned revolution that Chrysler started was in full swing, with GM and Ford both bringing out some of the zaniest cars. Newness sold cars, and Chrysler would not have anything new until 1960.

The 300F interior used four bucket seats, with tan leather standard. Redesigned dash was a bit on the flashy side.

The 300E featured a slightly different grille pattern and different hubcaps, but the most obvious change was the rear-end treatment. Overall, the design impressed people as being busier, but that was because the 300E shared the same body as the New Yorker. However, the E was by far the cleanest looking Chrysler. No heavy ornamentation here.

New features included such things as an optional Mirromatic rearview mirror that adjusted itself according to the rear backlight and breathable "Living Leather." An interesting feature was the swivel front seats that were supposed to facilitate entry and exit. The options list grew with items such as the automatic headlamp dimmer, Auto-Pilot (cruise control carried over from 1958) and True-Level Torsion-Aire air suspension. However, most optional axle ratios were eliminated—only a 2.93:1 ratio was available while standard was a 3.31:1. The optional 2½ inch exhaust system, manual transmission, manual steering and brakes were also eliminated.

Power steering, power brakes and the three-speed TorqueFlite automatic transmission were all standard equipment. Color choices remained at six (black, white, red, gray, tan and copper), and the interior was again finished in tan. Special-order colors and interior were available as well.

The biggest change on the 300E was the replacement of the 392 FirePower Hemi with a 380 hp 413 ci Golden Lion wedge-

Rare four-speed convertible. Rev counter's low position in the center console made it almost useless. *Tom Turner*

Long Ram 413 Wedge provided 375 healthy horses.

1959 Chrysler 300E	
Engine	
Type	V-8
Bore x stroke, in.	4.18 x 3.75
Displacement, cubic in.	413
Compression ratio	10.1:1
Horsepower	380@5000
Torque	450@3600
Chassis and drivetrain	
Transmission	3-spd automatic
Front suspension	Independent with torsion bars
Rear suspension	Live axle, leaf springs
Axle ratio	3.31:1
Brakes, front/rear	Drum/drum
General	
Wheelbase, in.	126
Height, in.	55.3 (55.7 convertible)
Width, in.	79.5
Length, in.	220.2
Weight, lb.	4,290 (4,350 convertible)
Performance	
0-60 mph	8.7
¼-mile e.t.@mph	17.2@92
Source	*Sports Car Illustrated, 8/1959*

head V-8. It featured dual Carter AFB carburetors and a camshaft that was a bit milder than the Hemi's. Low-end acceleration was better than that of the previous year's Hemi-powered 300D, but like most wedge engines, the 300E ran out of breath at higher rpm. At the Daytona, the best that an E could do was a lackluster 120.481 mph.

Still, the 300E was a better street car than any of its predecessors—quieter, smoother and far more tractable. Unfortunately, it failed to enthuse the buying public as production reached a low point of 550 hardtops

The 300G featured grille and rear-end styling changes. *Tom Turner*

and 140 convertibles. Of course, a list price of over $6,000 for an optioned-out 300E hardtop and of close to $6,500 for the convertible naturally limited sales because the cars just weren't that different from other Chrysler offerings. It must also be remembered that the new four-seater Thunderbird was selling well and that it was less expensive.

Prospects

Chrysler lost its styling leadership after 1959. The market moved away from fins, and the styling that Chrysler products had in the early 1960s was, with a few exceptions, awful.

That is why we can expect the 1955–59 300s to skyrocket in the near future. They represent a period when the Chrysler Corporation was definitely the styling and engineering leader in the industry.

Be aware that the 1957–59 Chryslers had the reputation of being rustbuckets. Be extra careful when you are considering investing in one of these beauties. Parts availability is poor, particularly for parts unique to the 300s. You can still find unrestored examples, and the reason they are still unrestored is lack of parts.

1960 300F

January 15, 1960, saw the introduction of the 300F, the sixth in the series. The horsepower race was on again: the 300F could be had with a 400 hp engine and a four-speed manual transmission. Chrysler got a lot of advertising mileage out of that offering because, according to most sources, it only built seven cars with the 400 hp engine. But they sure performed.

For example, the 300F bettered the Flying Mile record at Daytona (which previously stood at 139.37 mph set by a 300B) with a two-way average of 144.927 mph and a one-way run at 147.783 mph. For some serious

The interior, save for some minor trim changes, was essentially unchanged on the 300G. *Tom Turner*

numbers, Andy Granatelli entered a supercharged 300F at Bonneville and set a record of 184.049 mph and a one-way run at 189.990 mph. If you consider the poor aerodynamics of the 300F and its weight, these are tremendous figures.

The year 1960 was one of many changes. Most important was the introduction of unit construction or unibody on the entire Chrysler line, except for the Imperial. Simply put, rather than being the traditional body-on-frame construction, the body and chassis were now one welded unit to which the suspension and engine were attached. Advantages included a 100 percent improvement in rigidity which resulted in a tighter, quieter ride and ease of manufacture. However, rust

The 300H, shorn of fins, looked very similar to the 300G. This particular car has the rare dealer-installed 405 hp Short Ram 413 and Special Order (code 888) black leather interior.

was a much more serious problem in a unibody design, and this rusting out weakened the car's structural integrity.

Other engineering changes involved the 413 ci Golden Lion V-8. Although, as in 1959, two Carter AFB four-barrels were used, these were mounted on a unique ram induction setup designed to boost midrange torque. By shortening or lengthening tube length, Chrysler engineers were able to tailor to the engine's performance characteristics. The goal was to provide more power in the midrange for better passing. A thirty-inch-long tube was found to be optimum for these parameters. The standard engine thus produced 375 hp at 5200 rpm with 495 lb-ft of torque also at 5200 rpm.

The long ram tubes did have a drawback. They severely limited upper rpm performance. By having cut the internal length of the tubes to fifteen inches, the torque peak was raised to 3600 rpm on the optional 400 hp version. This enabled the engine to keep on pulling to 5200 rpm. Other improvements included larger exhaust valves (1.74 versus 1.60 inches), a solid lifter camshaft and a freer-flowing 2½ inch exhaust system. Acceleration times for 0–60 mph came in the

1960 Chrysler 300F	
Engine	
Type	V-8
Bore x stroke, in.	4.18 x 3.75
Displacement, cubic in.	413
Compression ratio	10.1:1 (10.1:1 opt.)
Horsepower	375@5000 (400@5200 opt.)
Torque	495@2800 (465@3600 opt.)
Chassis and drivetrain	
Transmission	3-spd automatic
Optional transmission	4-spd manual
Front suspension	Independent, torsion bars
Rear suspension	Live axle, leaf springs
Axle ratio	3.31:1
Brakes, front/rear	Drum/drum
General	
Wheelbase, in.	126
Height, in.	55.3 (55.7 convertible)
Width, in.	79.5
Length, in.	219.6
Weight, lb.	4,270 (4,310 convertible)
Performance (with 400 hp engine)	
0–60 mph	7.2
¼-mile e.t.@mph	NA
Source	Motor Life, 6/1960

low eight-second range and for the quarter-mile in the low sixteens for the 375 hp equipped 300F, while the 400 hp version took about a second off these times.

The standard transmission was the three-speed TorqueFlite with a 3.31:1 final drive ratio. The optional four-speed was only available as a package with the 400 hp engine. This was the Pont-a-Mousson aluminum unit used in the French Facel Vega, which had a Chrysler Hemi engine. An expensive $800 option on an already expensive car (about $6,000 with other options) limited its appeal and availability to seven units, including one convertible. But as I said before, it sure made good copy!

The styling, although showy, was dominated by the large, flared rear fins, a Continental-type trunk lid (dubbed the Toilet Seat) and a redesigned, serious-looking grille. Color choices were reduced to four: Formal Black, Toreador Red, Alaskan White and Terra Cotta. Other exterior and interior colors were available on a special-order basis.

Prospects

In spite of the great styling and performance, the 300F was not a great seller. Chrys-ler produced 964 hardtops and 248 convertibles. Few remain, with the convertible leading the way in terms of appreciation.

You can expect 300F prices to skyrocket because the 300F embodied the best of Virgil Exner's styling with great performance. Indeed, the 300F is a large, dominating car. Even with the ignition off, the 300F exudes a sense of raw power which is confirmed when the engine is turned on.

1961 300G

In 1961 the 300G appeared, a Letter car that was not too different from the 300F. The most noticeable change was the front grille; basically the 300F grille was turned

The 300H interior.

1961 Chrysler 300G	
Engine	
Type	V-8
Bore x stroke, in.	4.18 x 3.75
Displacement, cubic in.	413
Compression ratio	10.1:1
Horsepower	375@5000
Torque	495@2800
Chassis and drivetrain	
Transmission	3-spd automatic
Optional transmission	3-spd manual
Front suspension	Independent, torsion bars
Rear suspension	Live axle, leaf springs
Axle ratio	3.31:1
Brakes, front/rear	Drum/drum
General	
Wheelbase, in.	126
Height, in.	55.6 (56 convertible)
Width, in.	79.4
Length, in.	219.8
Weight, lb.	4,260 (4,315 convertible)
Performance (with 3-spd manual)	
0-60 mph	8.3
¼-mile e.t.@mph	NA
Source	*Motor Trend*, 6/1961

upside down and the quad headlights were slanted inward as on the 1960 Lincoln. The grille change diluted some of the tough-guy look, and the rear styling was somewhat busier, although the Continental spare had disappeared.

Still, the 300G was the last example of the waning Exner Forward Look fins. By this time, Chrysler had lost the styling leadership earned in the late 1950s, and some of the 1961 models were truly "different," to say the least.

Basically, the 300G was a carryover. The 375 hp Long Ram engine was standard, but the 400 hp Short Ram now came with a three-speed manual (non-synchro first) that was also available on the Lancers and Valiants. We do not know how many 300Gs so equipped were built, but it cannot have been more than a handful.

One interesting feature on all Chrysler V-8s was the switch from a generator to an alternator; in 1960, only the 400 hp engine was equipped with an alternator. Also wheel size was increased from fourteen to fifteen inches, which improved handling.

The interior was still finished in tan leather, although the pattern was somewhat different from that in the 300F. Exterior colors were limited to four: Formal Black, Mardi Gras Red, Cinnamon and Alaskan White.

Prospects

Production reached 1,280 for the hardtop and 337 for the convertible. These low numbers ensure the G's collectibility, but it is also important to remember that the 300G was the last Letter car that did not share the 300 designation with other Chryslers.

1962 300H

The year 1962 saw many changes; most obvious were those in the styling department with an end to the fins. But the front grille design was basically a carryover from the 300G, as was the interior. The 300H was now built on a shorter 122 inch wheelbase from the Newport rather than on the 126 inch New Yorker platform. This resulted in improved performance as the H was about 300 pounds lighter, although it can be argued that the ride suffered somewhat.

A 300H convertible, a very rare car with only 123 built. *Ron Wenger*

Performance, however, was excellent. The standard engine was a 380 hp 413 featuring inline-mounted dual four-barrel Carters, providing better than the usual Letter Series performance: 0–60 mph in the high seven-second range and the quarter-mile time in the low fifteens.

For the performance enthusiast, a rare 405 hp version of the 413 was available as a dealer-installed option. This was a Short Ram version with a nasty solid lifter cam and an 11.1:1 compression ratio. Even on a warm day, it took about fifteen minutes of idling (or trying to keep it idling) before it ran on its own. Performance was impressive: 0–60 mph in the high sixes and quarter-mile times in the 14.7 range.

A modified 300H with the 405 hp engine was entered in the 1962 Winternationals. Best times included an elapsed time of 12.88 seconds and a speed of 108.40 mph. This particular car had the TorqueFlite transmission, a 4.56:1 axle, headers and the usual drag-racing modifications to encourage proper weight transfer.

An Andy Granatelli 300H turned 189.9 mph at Bonneville with the help of two McCulloch Superchargers and also set the Flying Mile record at 179.472 mph. Very fast indeed.

Standard transmission was the Torque-Flite automatic with a three-speed manual optional. Either transmission was available with the 405 hp engine as it was a dealer-installed option.

The interior was finished in the usual tan leather, but other colors were available under special order.

Prospects

Sales hit an all time low with the 300H: 435 hardtops and only 123 convertibles. I doubt if more than seventy-five 300Hs have survived. If you are interested in a 300H with the 405 hp engine, you must make sure that it is an original dealer-installed unit and that means documentation. Look for appreciation to be quite strong simply because so few have survived, especially in the convertible.

1963 300J

The 1963 Chrysler line was totally redesigned under the direction of Elwood Engel, who replaced Virgil Exner. Engel, hired from Ford, was responsible for the restyled 1961 Lincoln and Thunderbird. The new Chrysler look was dubbed the "Crisp, Clean, Custom Look." Still, the Exner influence was there—for example, the large trapezoidal grille and large wheelwell cutouts—and it wasn't until the 1965 model year before Exner's influence finally vanished.

1962 Chrysler 300H	
Engine	
Type	V-8
Bore x stroke, in.	4.18 x 3.75
Displacement, cubic in.	413
Compression ratio	10.0:1
Horsepower	380@5200
Torque	485@3200
Optional engine	405 hp 413 cid (dealer-installed)
Chassis and drivetrain	
Transmission	3-spd automatic
Front suspension	Independent, torsion bars
Rear suspension	Live axle, leaf springs
Axle ratio	3.23:1
Brakes, front/rear	Drum/drum
General	
Wheelbase, in.	122
Height, in.	55.2
Width, in.	79.4
Length, in.	214.9
Weight, lb.	4,240

Short Ram 405 hp 413. Tall air cleaner studs were designed to accommodate taller air cleaner elements required with the 405. Power brake booster was relocated in cavity of left front fender.

The 300J continued the tradition that started with the C300: a powerful engine mated to a roadworthy chassis luxuriously appointed. The 300J still came with a leather interior as standard equipment and with five exterior color choices: Formal Black, Alabaster, Madison Grey, Claret and Oyster White.

Performance was good too, with a 390 hp 413 featuring the Short Ram Induction setup. No optional engine was available, but a three-speed manual was an option in lieu of the standard heavy-duty TorqueFlite automatic.

However, to the dismay of the motoring press, the suspension was softened as can be seen by the table below.

Ride rate at wheel	300G	300H	300J
Front, lb/in.	160	130	125
Rear, lb/in.	190	160	150

Soft suspension tends to produce a more comfortable ride at the expense of cornering capability. However, you can easily compensate for softer springs by installing much heavier shock absorbers. In fact, current guidelines for combining handling and ride call for relatively soft springs with firm shocks and large diameter front and rear

A 1963 300J with horizontal headlights and round taillights. Still sleek and elegant without any side adornments. *Don Drakulich and Ron Wenger*

sway bars. The cars listed above all came with a 0.75 inch front sway bar.

Firmer shock absorbers should not hurt originality for those enthusiasts who still enjoy driving their cars, and the same can be said of modern tires and rear sway bars, unless the car is strictly a show car.

There were some changes made to the J's brakes; Bendix brakes replaced Chrysler's center-plane brakes and proved to be more resistant to fade. A foot pedal actuated the parking brakes.

Prospects

Although the tradition continued with the 300J, sales hit an abysmal low of 400 units, all hardtops. Perhaps the $1,700 differential between the J and a non-Letter 300 adversely affected sales, and Chrysler's lack of promotion certainly did not help.

In spite of the fact that so few 300Js remain, the prospect for appreciation is modest simply because the Letter Series by 1963 had lost its exclusivity and prestige. If the earlier Letter cars rise in value, so too will the 300J, but don't expect the J to rise simply on its own.

1964 300K

The 1964 300K made a comeback, at least in terms of sales: 3,022 hardtops and 625 convertibles. This success probably reflected a $1,000 reduction of the list price. The leather interior was replaced by vinyl (leather

1963 Chrysler 300J	
Engine	
Type	V-8
Bore x stroke, in.	4.18 x 3.75
Displacement, cubic in.	413
Compression ratio	9.6:1
Horsepower	390@4800
Torque	485@3600
Chassis and drivetrain	
Transmission	3-spd automatic
Front suspension	Independent, torsion bars
Rear suspension	Live axle, leaf springs
Axle ratio	3.23:1
Brakes, front/rear	Drum/drum
General	
Wheelbase, in.	122
Height, in.	55.6
Width, in.	79
Length, in.	215.5
Weight, lb.	4,235
Performance (with 400 hp engine)	
0-60 mph	7.5
¼-mile e.t.@mph	15.4@94
Source	*Car and Driver,* 4/1963

was optional) and the standard 413 engine featured a single four-barrel. Chrysler also advertised the car more extensively.

The standard 413 pumped out 360 hp while the optional Short Ram-equipped K put out 390 horses. Wheel size reverted to a fourteen-inch rim with an 8.00x14 standard tire. On the Short Ram engine tires were 8.50x14s, which were an option on the lower horsepower engine as well.

A 1964 300K convertible.

The 300K interior gave the impression of having four bucket seats, but could seat five.

1964 Chrysler 300K

Engine
Type	V-8
Bore x stroke, in.	4.18 x 3.75
Displacement, cubic in.	413
Compression ratio	9.6:1
Horsepower	360@4600
Torque	470@3200

Chassis and drivetrain
Transmission	3-spd automatic
Optional transmission	4-spd manual
Front suspension	Independent, torsion bars
Rear suspension	Live axle, leaf springs
Axle ratio	3.23:1
Brakes, front/rear	Drum/drum

General
Wheelbase, in.	122
Height, in.	55.3
Width, in.	79
Length, in.	215.3
Weight, lb.	4,250

Interestingly, Chrysler made available a new four-speed manual transmission; however only eighty-four cars were equipped with it. The shift lever was uniquely located: it was on the floor to the left of the console rather than at the center of the console. The standard TorqueFlite no longer used push buttons; instead, the driver selected gears with a console-mounted shifter. Both the automatic and manual transmissions used the same final drive ratio, 3.23:1.

A 120 mph speedometer replaced the 150 mph unit, and the tachometer became optional. A tilt steering wheel was offered for the first time, and color choices expanded to sixteen.

Prospects

From the enthusiast's point of view, all these changes represented a further watering down of the 300's original concept. Still, it was a better car than the non-Letter 300, and in spite of the fact that more 300Ks were built than any other Letter Series, few remain.

A 300K convertible with optional leather and 390 hp engine is probably the most desirable from a collector's point of view. Look for clean restored examples rather

Only 84 300Ks came with a four-speed manual transmission. *Tom Smith*

than investing in a K that needs restoration. Parts availability is poor. Although the 300K has less glamour associated with it than do earlier 300s, it is a solid investment because from mechanical and styling points of view it still has the luxury and performance associated with a Letter Series car, and just as important, a K bears the Virgil Exner imprint.

1965 300L

There were many reasons for the demise of the Letter Series. Sales were never that good, and Chrysler could not have made much money on the line. Since 1962 when the non-Letter 300s appeared, the impact of the Letter Series as a means of increasing sales had diminished considerably. Performance did sell cars, but by 1962 the emphasis was on the intermediates. It seemed that if you were a car manufacturer, all you had to

1965 Chrysler 300L

Engine

Type	V-8
Bore x stroke, in.	4.18 x 3.75
Displacement, cubic in.	413
Compression ratio	10.1:1
Horsepower	360@4800
Torque	470@3200

Chassis and drivetrain

Transmission	3-spd automatic
Optional transmission	4-spd manual
Front suspension	Independent, torsion bars
Rear suspension	Live axle, leaf springs
Axle ratio	3.23:1
Brakes, front/rear	Drum/drum

General

Wheelbase, in.	124
Height, in.	55.3
Width, in.	79.5
Length, in.	218.2
Weight, lb.	4,660

Performance

0-60 mph	8.8
¼-mile e.t.@mph	17.3@82
Source	*Motor Trend*, 3/1965

Not all 300s are restored to original condition. This 300K sees action at Road Atlanta. *Ted Dalack*

do was put your biggest, most powerful engine in your least expensive platform, give this creation a catchy name and watch sales go. Luxury options just made the Letter car too expensive and thus out of range of the exploding youth market. The Letter Series had the reputation of being big highway cruisers. Now, quarter-mile times were more important.

The 1965 300L was based on a completely redesigned body. It was handsome but bore little resemblance to previous Letter cars. Engine choice was limited to a single four-barrel 413 rated at 360 hp with either a standard TorqueFlite automatic or an optional four-speed manual. In either case, the 3.23:1 rear was the only one available. Vinyl was the standard material for the interior, while leather was optional. Car buyers chose from many exterior colors, and for those so inclined, a full vinyl roof was available.

Gone were the days of Daytona and the Speed Trials. The 300L could go from 0–60 mph in the high eight-second range, respectable for a full-size car.

Prospects

Production was relatively high: 2,405 hardtops and 440 convertibles. You can expect these 300Ls to appreciate, although perhaps not quite as rapidly as do earlier Letter Series, but they are definitely the most desirable 1965 Chryslers.

The 300L, last of the line. *Don Rook*

Chapter 3

★★	**1962-71 300 sedans**
★★★	**1962-70 300 convertible**
★★★↘	**1963 Pacesetter convertible**
★★★	**1963 Silver 300**
★★★	**1970 300-H**
★★	**1979 Cordoba 300**

1962–79 Chrysler 300

Beginning with the 1962 model year, Chrysler introduced the non-Letter 300 Series as a replacement for the Windsor series. From a marketing point of view, this was a success. Over 25,000 non-Letter 300s were sold in 1962. The real surprise is that Chrysler resisted doing this earlier.

There is no question that the Letter Series had been Chrysler's primary image car, which had earned the reputation of being

Non-Letter 300s from 1962 to 1971 were available in four-door form. This is a 1963.

The 1962 Chrysler 300 captured the feeling and
elan of the much more expensive Letter Series.
This is a four-door hardtop. *Willard Stein*

the car to own—not only for performance but also for status. Limited production, high price, luxury and high performance made it the premier Chrysler offering for many years. How you reacted to the new 300 Series depended on your point of view. The enthusiast was disappointed because his new 300 would not embody the exclusiveness of the Letter Series 300. But the 300 certainly had moved within the reach of more customers—and that is the whole purpose of manufacturing cars.

Unfortunately, auto manufacturers fail to realize the value that a limited-production car generates in terms of goodwill and image. They appear to base the decision to continue production solely on whether or not the car is profitable and sells in large quantity.

1962-71 300

The 1962 300 was called the Sport Series; it consisted of a two-door hardtop, a four-door hardtop and a convertible. This basic offering continued until 1971, the last model year that the 300 was offered, with the

exception of the convertible that was available until 1970. The standard engine was a 305 hp 383, with a 340 hp and 380 hp 413 optional. The 380 hp version was the same engine that was standard equipment on the

Probably the most desirable of the non-Letter 300s is this 1963 Pacesetter convertible. *D. G. Shingledecker*

This sorry example is a 1964 Silver 300K. The Silver 300 package was available on regular Chrysler 300s (two-door only) and the 300K. Silver paint, black leather interior and black vinyl roof made the Silver 300 stand out.

1966 Chrysler 300	
Engine	
Type	V-8
Bore x stroke, in.	4.32 x 3.75
Displacement, cubic in.	440
Compression ratio	10.1:1
Horsepower	365@4600
Torque	480@3200
Chassis and drivetrain	
Transmission	3-spd automatic
Front suspension	Independent, torsion bars
Rear suspension	Live axle, leaf springs
Axle ratio	3.23:1
Brakes, front/rear	Disc/drum
General	
Wheelbase, in.	124
Height, in.	54.6
Width, in.	79.5
Length, in.	221.9
Weight, lb.	4,340
Performance	
0-60 mph	7.8
¼-mile e.t.@mph	17.3@84.5
Source	*Car and Driver*, 11/1965

300H. The theory was that you could option out a regular 300 to have the same performance as a Letter car, but at a considerable savings. Even so, differences between the non-Letter and Letter versions became apparent on the road. Visually, you discerned little difference between the two.

The only difference between the 300 and 300H was the letter H on the trunk lid and the 300H's use of fifteen-inch wheels with a different wheel cover.

You can expect slow, yet steady appreciation. The non-Letter 300s will never be

Most desirable of the 1965–68 non-Letter 300s are the convertibles. These are 1966s. *Don Rook*

worth as much as a Letter car, but they are and will be more affordable. The convertible, as can be seen from the production figures at the back of the book, will definitely appreciate at a faster pace because production in any given year never exceeded 2,000 units.

Convertibles are more difficult to restore; get the best restoration that you can afford.

The 1963 300 Sport Series continued in the same vein. Sales were good, and interestingly, engine horsepower ratings surpassed those of the 300Js. Standard was the 305 hp 383, but optional engines included four-

The last of the pre-fuselage styling 300s is the 1968, as exemplified by this gorgeous convertible. *Chuck Angel*

Non-Letter 300s provided big car ride, but with tighter handling and acceleration than Chrys-ler's other big car offerings. This is a 1968 four-door. *Michael Shingledecker*

barrel 413s rated at 360 hp and 365 hp, a four-barrel 426 wedge rated at 373 hp and two Short Ram versions rated at 415 and 425 hp. This was as high as horsepower ratings would get in the Sport Series. Any 1963 300 with the 426 engine is not only rare, but more desirable as well.

The Pacesetter 300 was a trim package available only on the convertible and two-door hardtop in late 1963. It came in special color combinations and was distinguished by checkered flags beneath the 300 emblem. A Silver 300 was also available, only on the two-door hardtop (and on the 300K). The Silver came with a black leather and vinyl interior, and a black vinyl roof that ended where the rear roof pillars began.

Besides the styling changes and the dropping of the Sport designation, there wasn't much difference on the 1964 non-Letter 300s. Engine choice was now limited to one: a 360 hp 413 that provided adequate acceleration.

The year 1965 brought the redesigned Chrysler line great success; over 200,000 units were sold. These cars were longer,

sleeker and attractive to boot. Clearly a break with the past, the Engel-designed models brought Chrysler Corporation into the 1960s.

The 300 in 1965 came standard with a 315 hp 383, while 340 hp and 360 hp 413s were optional. All these engines came with a single four-barrel carburetor. No special models or trim packages were available.

In 1966 the 300s got larger displacement engines. The 413, bored 0.13 inches, now yielded 440 ci and 350 hp (365 hp at mid-year). The standard engine was a 325 hp 383.

Optional, and more interesting, was the 440 TNT engine. Rated at 375 hp, this engine featured a twin-snorkel air cleaner, a stronger camshaft and valvetrain, and a free-flowing dual exhaust system with 2¼ inch interior diameter exhaust pipes. Included with the engine were a heavy-duty suspension and fifteen-inch wheels, which were necessary to clear the front disc brakes, also part of the package.

Performance with this big V-8 wasn't bad, considering the car weighed over 4,500 lb. without passengers. Although 0–60 mph

1969 Chrysler 300

Engine
Type	V-8
Bore x stroke, in.	4.32 x 3.75
Displacement, cubic in.	440
Compression ratio	10.1:1
Horsepower	350@4400
Torque	480@2800

Chassis and drivetrain
Transmission	3-spd automatic
Front suspension	Independent, torsion bars
Rear suspension	Live axle, leaf springs
Axle ratio	3.23:1
Brakes, front/rear	Disc/drum

General
Wheelbase, in.	124
Height, in.	55
Width, in.	79
Length, in.	225
Weight, lb.	4,450

Performance
0-60 mph	8.5
¼-mile e.t.@mph	16.1@86.3
Source	*Car Life*, 9/1969

Convertibles on the new body style were built only during 1969–70. This is a 1969. *Bob McVoy*

came in the low eight-second range, from 60 mph on, the engine pooped out a bit. For example, the 300J could reach 100 mph in about 17.5 seconds, but it took the TNT-powered 300 over twenty-six seconds.

The 300's forte was effortless high-speed cruising. It was your family car with a little more oomph and better handling.

The years 1967 and 1968 saw further refinement, at least in styling. The 1968 ver-

Optional 440 TNT was worth a few horsepower and sported this distinctive dual-snorkel air cleaner.

The 1970 300 Hurst combined performance and luxury in a big car configuration. *Roman Robaszewski*

sions are particularly attractive because of a new grille that featured hidden headlights. The 440 engine remained standard equipment with the TNT package optional.

In 1969 a complete restyle, dubbed the fuselage look, appeared. These cars featured smooth but bulging sides and a loop-type front bumper. Though not bad looking at all, the styling did emphasize and exaggerate the car's massive size.

The fuselage look continued until the 300's demise in 1971. Chrysler really made no effort to relate performance and everything else that the numbers 300 had once stood for. The 300 was a luxurious big car.

Hood emblem shows the familiar Hurst "H."

1970 300-H

As far as non-Letter 300s go, however, the 1970 300-H stands out. This was a specially modified 300 two-door hardtop. Hurst Performance Corporation undertook the modifications that were primarily cosmetic in nature. All 300-Hs came in one color, Spinnaker White with Sauterne Mist Gold accents (a GM color), and all used a special

The 440 TNT was the only engine available on the 300 Hurst. *Roman Robaszewski*

Leather seats from the Imperial rounded out the
300 Hurst. *Roman Robaszewski*

Last of the 300s is this 1971. *Ray Doern*

fiberglass hood and a trunk lid that had a molded-in spoiler. The interior, taken from the two-door Imperial, was finished in tan leather.

Only one engine was available, the 375 hp 440 mated to a three-speed TorqueFlite automatic. Heavy-duty suspension, H70x15 tires on Chrysler road wheels and the usual luxury options rounded out the package. To have had the car perform according to the image it projected would have required the 426 Hemi, and it was originally conceived this way. However, according to Chrysler engineers, too many modifications would have had to have been made to the engine compartment. Too bad.

Production figures vary. Five hundred were supposed to have been built, but estimates range from 400 to 650. The most accepted figure is 503, which includes two convertibles and one car equipped with a sunroof.

Prospects

In spite of its Hurst heritage and historical significance, the 300-H is undervalued at about $6,000 for a clean example. If you are interested in a 300-H, do not, by any means, buy an unrestored example that is missing the unique hood and trunk lid; it will be almost impossible to locate others.

1979 Cordoba 300

The 300 designation surfaced briefly in 1979 on a Chrysler Cordoba equipped with an optional Chrysler 300 package. This was a complete chassis, powertrain and appearance package that was fairly faithful to the original 300 concept as interpreted by 1979 standards and limitations.

The Cordoba 300 was powered by a four-barrel DMAC exhaust 360 V-8 rated at 195 hp (190 hp in California). It was available only in a Spinnaker White exterior with a red leather and vinyl interior. The most desirable of a long list of options was the T-bar roof.

Perhaps the timing was not quite right for this car because only 4,292 were built. Chrysler built 756 for the Canadian market, and seven of these were painted Chianti Red.

The 1979 Chrysler 300 is a good-looking car. Although it lacks the sheer brute power

The 1979 Chrysler 300 at least revived the spirit of the great Letter Series 300s. *Dale Burkhardt*

The 360 V-8 loaded down with emission controls put out 195 hp. *Dale Burkhardt*

1970 Chrysler 300-H	
Engine	
Type	V-8
Bore x stroke, in.	4.32 x 3.75
Displacement, cubic in.	440
Compression ratio	9.7:1
Horsepower	375@4600
Torque	480@3200
Chassis and drivetrain	
Transmission	3-spd automatic
Front suspension	Independent, torsion bars
Rear suspension	Live axle, leaf springs
Axle ratio	3.23:1
Brakes, front/rear	Disc/drum
General	
Wheelbase, in.	124
Height, in.	54.7
Width, in.	79
Length, in.	224.7
Weight, lb.	4,480
Performance	
0–60 mph	NA
¼-mile e.t.@mph	16.8@87.3
Source	*Road Test*, 7/1970

of the early Letter cars, it is a better handling car.

Prospects

The non-Letter 300s, although they lack the glamour and rarity of the Letter cars, still represent a good way to get into the hobby, particularly from your wallet's point of view. Because they were built in relatively large quantities, you will be able to purchase a parts car or two if you are planning to restore a basket case, but you are much better off getting a car that is already restored. The convertibles are good looking and will appreciate at a faster pace. Look for loaded-to-the-hilt models rather than strippers or cars equipped with odd options and color combinations.

1956–58 Plymouth Fury

If you are looking for a fifties Plymouth with lots of pizzaz, there is really only one that you can consider. The 1956-58 Furys were distinctive automobiles that combined excellent performance with a unique and exciting visual package. The Fury was to Plymouth what the 300 was to Chrysler.

1956-58

Capitalizing on the momentum created by the revitalized styling of 1955, Plymouth brought out the Fury as a midyear introduction on January 10, 1956. Based on the two-door hardtop Belvedere, it was nevertheless distinctive. The one available color, an off-white, was set off effectively by a gold anodized bodyside sweepspear. Gold was also used in the grille and on the wheel covers. All 1956-58 Furys sported this color combination.

Unlike its Chrysler 300B and DeSoto Adventurer counterparts, the Fury was not

1956 Plymouth Fury	
Engine	
Type	V-8
Bore x stroke, in.	3.81 x 3.31
Displacement, cubic in.	303
Compression ratio	9.25:1
Horsepower	240@4800
Torque	310@2800
Chassis and drivetrain	
Transmission	3-spd manual
Optional transmission	2-spd automatic
Front suspension	Independent, coil springs
Rear suspension	Live axle, leaf springs
Axle ratio	3.73:1
Brakes, front/rear	Drum/drum
General	
Wheelbase, in.	115
Height, in.	58.8
Width, in.	74.6
Length, in.	204.8
Weight, lb.	3,650

1957 Plymouth Fury	
Engine	
Type	V-8
Bore x stroke, in.	3.91 x 3.31
Displacement, cubic in.	318
Compression ratio	9.25:1
Horsepower	290@5400
Torque	325@4000
Chassis and drivetrain	
Transmission	3-spd manual
Optional transmission	3-spd automatic
Front suspension	Independent, torsion bars
Rear suspension	Live axle, leaf springs
Axle ratio	3.73:1
Brakes, front/rear	Drum/drum
General	
Wheelbase, in.	118
Height, in.	53.5
Width, in.	79.4
Length, in.	206
Weight, lb.	3,595

1958 Plymouth Fury

Engine

Type	V-8 (carbureted 350 V-8 opt.)
Bore x stroke, in.	3.91 x 3.31 (4.06 x 3.38 opt.)
Displacement, cubic in.	318 (350 opt.)
Compression ratio	9.25:1 (10.0:1 opt.)
Horsepower	290@5400 (305@5000 opt.)
Torque	325@4000 (370@3600 opt.)

Chassis and drivetrain

Transmission	3-spd manual
Optional transmission	3-spd automatic
Front suspension	Independent, torsion bars
Rear suspension	Live axle, leaf springs
Brakes, front/rear	Drum/drum

General

Wheelbase, in.	118
Height, in.	53.5
Width, in.	79.4
Length, in.	206
Weight, lb.	3,510

powered by a Hemi-head engine. Instead, a 303 ci Hy-Fire V-8 with polyspheric combustion chambers was used. In this kind of combustion chamber design, the cylinder head is relatively shallow and the piston design determines the combustion chamber shape. A rating of 240 hp was reached through the use of a 9.25:1 compression ratio, a solid lifter cam, four-barrel carburetor and a free-flowing exhaust system. Naturally, the Fury came with heavy-duty springs and shocks, but the Fury sat an inch lower than other Plymouths. An inch may not be much, but it makes a big difference in the way the car looks—purposeful.

A preproduction Fury ran at Daytona that year with a Flying Mile time of 124 mph. On

The 1956 Plymouth Fury added some excitement to the usual staid Plymouth line-up. *Thomas Ray*

the street, the Fury could reach 60 mph in the mid-nine-second range and the quarter-mile time in the low seventeens. A three-speed manual was standard, and the two-speed PowerFlite automatic was optional. Other optional equipment included power brakes, steering, seat and windows, and air conditioning.

Perhaps the reason the Fury was not equipped with a Hemi was that it would have blown the doors off of the 300B. Built on a 115 inch wheelbase, the Fury weighed hundreds of pounds less than the 300B, and you just couldn't have a Fury that was faster than the car that was the company's most prestigious and one of its most expensive. Plymouth built and sold low-priced cars, and the Fury's base price was $2,866, which helps to account for sales of 4,485 units.

If 1956 was successful, then the 1957 was an absolute smash. Chrysler restyled the entire line under the eye of Virgil Exner and took the styling lead from General Motors. The 1957 Fury was longer, lower, wider and much sleeker than the 1956.

Besides the new styling, the Fury benefited from the torsion bar front suspension, and optional TorqueFlite automatic transmission. Optional equipment remained nearly the same as in 1963, but the 303 was now bored to 318 ci and named the V-800. Two four-barrel carbs helped to raise horsepower to 290, and performance improved accordingly. Sales, too, hit a high of 7,438.

The 1958 version was restyled slightly including four headlights, matching under-bumper grille and smaller taillights. The V-800 was standard, while a new Golden

Commando 350 ci wedge was optional. Rated at 305 hp, it too sported two four-barrel carburetors.

A 315 hp version was also available; it used fuel injection, the same ill-fated system that was used on the 300D. Most, if not all, were later reconverted to carburetors. Production for the 1958 reached 5,303.

The year 1959 marked the end of the Fury as a limited-production high-performance automobile. The name Fury was used on an entire line, although a Sports Fury model was available as a hardtop and convertible, but that did not last into 1960.

Prospects

Prospects are good for the 1956-58 Furys. Relatively unknown, they have been overshadowed by the 300 Letter Series, so you should be able to find a nice example in the $5,000 to $7,000 range. Although Furys lack the exclusivity of a 300, they are prime examples of Virgil Exner at his best, and for this reason you can expect strong appreciation. Considering the relatively high production run, not many Furys have survived into the 1980s, and as with all late 1950s Chrysler products, watch out for rust.

The 240 hp version of the 303 ci Hy-Fire V-8 was standard equipment. *Thomas Ray*

The dash, by 1950 standards, was relatively simple. This Fury has optional air conditioning. *Thomas Ray*

The 290 hp 318 with dual quads made the Fury the quickest 1957 Plymouth. *Dale Frahm*

For 1957, the Fury had a much cleaner, lighter grille. The rather elegant side spears contrib-uted to the car's sleekness while emphasizing the rear fins. *Dale Frahm*

For 1958, the Fury was relatively unchanged.
Note delicate, almost frail looking roof. *Norman Buelow*

Front grille featured some minor changes—
most obvious were the lower grille's horizontal
bars. The taillights, too, were changed slightly.

Both 1957 and 1958 Furys featured beautifully
styled bumpers, unlike the battering rams of
today's cars. *Norman Buelow*

Interior was functionally simple. This Fury has a manual transmission. *Norman Buelow*

The 305 hp 350 ci Golden Commando provided lots of low-end torque for the 1958 Fury. Valve covers and air cleaners were painted gold. *Norman Buelow*

Chapter 5

1956–60 DeSoto Adventurer

In the marketing scheme, the DeSoto was Chrysler's Oldsmobile, competing in the medium-price field. GM consisted of Chevrolet, Pontiac, Oldsmobile, Buick and Cadillac. Chrysler's complementary offerings were Plymouth, Dodge, DeSoto, Chrysler and Imperial. Sales in the 1950s were decent; in some years DeSoto outsold Chrysler. However, unlike its sister divisions, DeSoto was not able to bounce back from the 1958 recession. The year 1957 saw 126,514 DeSotos produced, 1958 production dropped to 49,445 and by 1960 a dismal 26,081 units were built. An abbreviated 1961 model run saw an additional 3,034 units. Without any great fanfare, an announcement on November 18, 1960, indicated that production would cease by the month's end. The DeSoto had lost its appeal.

Still, from a collector's point of view, there are some bright moments, namely the Adventurer, introduced as a midyear entry on February 18, 1956, and the Pacesetter convertible that preceded the Adventurer by about a month.

1956 Pacesetter

DeSoto was selected to pace the 1956 Indianapolis 500 race. As now, this meant lots of publicity, and to take full advantage of it, DeSoto produced a special Pacesetter convertible. Based on the Fireflite convertible, the Pace cars were available only in white accented by lots of gold: gold wheel covers, gold top and side sweeps, gold vinyl upholstery, gold instrument panel, ivory and gold steering wheel and gold threads in the black carpets. Even in the age of flash, this combination stood out.

The powertrain consisted of a DeSoto 330 ci Hemi sporting a single four-barrel carburetor, rated at 255 hp. The PowerFlite automatic transmission was standard equipment. The rest of the car, mechanically, was standard Fireflite.

Prospects

Most Pacesetter convertibles were equipped with luxury options, such as power seats and power windows. Most sources list that between 100 and 200 examples were built. According to the National DeSoto Club, however, the true figure may be closer to 400. Incredibly, few have survived; not more than twenty-five or so are known to remain. Definitely a good bet for appreciation.

1956-60 Adventurer

The Adventurer was similar to the Pace cars in terms of styling; however, it was only

The 1956 Pace Car convertible put the spotlight on DeSoto. Note prominent dual exhausts and triple taillights. *Gus DeGazio*

available as a hardtop in 1956. Color choice was more varied: three colors, gold, black and white were available in six combinations.

Considerably more powerful, the Adventurer used a dual four-barrel 341 ci Hemi

1956 DeSoto Adventurer	
Engine	
Type	V-8
Bore x stroke, in.	3.78 x 3.80
Displacement, cubic in.	341
Compression ratio	9.25:1
Horsepower	320@5200
Torque	NA
Chassis and drivetrain	
Transmission	3-spd automatic
Front suspension	Independent, coil springs
Rear suspension	Live axle, leaf springs
Axle ratio	3.73:1
Brakes, front/rear	Drum/drum
General	
Wheelbase, in.	126
Height, in.	58
Length, in.	220.9
Weight, lb.	3,870

that pumped out 320 hp, only 20 hp less than the standard Chrysler 300B engine. The Adventurer's engine benefited from a 9.25:1 compression ratio, a high-lift camshaft, larger cylinder head ports and performance-oriented intake manifold and ignition timing. It was a strong, durable engine. A prototype ran 137 mph at Daytona, and later the same car ran 144 mph at the Chrysler Proving Grounds. The Adventurer provided 300B performance, perhaps not in the same understated way, but at a much lower cost. Production in 1956 was a low 996 units.

DeSoto shared in all the improvements made for the 1957 model year: TorqueFlite transmission, front torsion bar suspension and, of course, styling. DeSoto benefited from the masterly touch of Virgil Exner, who in that year was elevated to a newly created position of vice president, director of styling.

The Adventurer Series looked great, especially as a convertible (in addition to the two-door hardtop). Also befitting the flagship that it was, the Adventurer received a 345 ci Hemi that boasted 345 hp, one for each cubic inch. The Chevrolet Corvette and the Chrysler 300B also had engines that boasted one horsepower per cubic inch in 1957, but these were optional engines, not

Single four-barrel Fireflite provided plenty of oomph. *Gus DeGazio*

standard as the Adventurer's was. Unfortunately, this was the last year the Hemi engine was available. Production reached 1,650 for the hardtop and 300 for the convertible.

The 1958 Adventurer was essentially the same car. Again introduced two months later than the rest of the DeSoto line, it featured a minor facelift. However, mechanically, the Hemi was replaced by a two four-barrel 350 ci wedge, the Turboflash V-8, rated at 345 hp. Low-end performance was similar to the Hemi's but midrange and upper rpm performance was noticeably poorer. A 355 hp version, however, was

1957 DeSoto Adventurer	
Engine	
Type	V-8
Bore x stroke, in.	3.80 x 3.80
Displacement, cubic in.	345
Compression ratio	9.25:1
Horsepower	345@5200
Torque	355@3600
Chassis and drivetrain	
Transmission	3-spd automatic
Front suspension	Independent, torsion bars
Rear suspension	Live axle, leaf springs
Axle ratio	3.73:1
Brakes, front/rear	Drum/drum
General	
Wheelbase, in.	126
Height, in.	55
Width, in.	78.2
Length, in.	218
Weight, lb.	4,040

The 1956 Adventurer hardtop. Gold anodized wheel covers set it off. The 1956 Plymouth Fury used the same wheel cover, but without the DeSoto script. *Larry Zappone*

available as an option. This engine featured the Bendix fuel injection system that was tried on other Chrysler engines, with the same poor results. All were recalled to have the unreliable fuel injection replaced with carburetors.

1958 DeSoto Adventurer	
Engine	
Type	V-8
Bore x stroke, in.	4.12 x 3.38
Displacement, cubic in.	361
Compression ratio	10.25:1
Horsepower	345@5000
Torque	400@3600
Chassis and drivetrain	
Transmission	3-spd automatic
Front suspension	Independent, torsion bars
Rear suspension	Live axle, leaf springs
Axle ratio	3.31:1
Brakes, front/rear	Drum/drum
General	
Wheelbase, in.	126
Height, in.	55
Width, in.	78.2
Length, in.	218.6
Weight, lb.	4,000

1959 DeSoto Adventurer	
Engine	
Type	V-8
Bore x stroke, in.	4.25 x 3.38
Displacement, cubic in.	383
Compression ratio	10.1:1
Horsepower	350@5000
Torque	425@3600
Chassis and drivetrain	
Transmission	3-spd automatic
Front suspension	Independent, torsion bars
Rear suspension	Live axle, leaf springs
Axle ratio	3.31:1
Brakes, front/rear	Drum/drum
General	
Wheelbase, in.	126
Height, in.	55
Width, in.	78.7
Length, in.	221.1
Weight, lb.	3,980

Except for the somewhat busy triple taillights, the rear end is pleasingly simple. *Larry Zappone*

1960 DeSoto Adventurer

Engine

Type	V-8
Bore x stroke, in.	4.25 x 3.38
Displacement, cubic in.	383
Compression ratio	10.1:1
Horsepower	305@4600
Torque	410@2400
Optional engine	383-4bbl, 383 Ramcharger

Chassis and drivetrain

Transmission	3-spd automatic
Front suspension	Independent, torsion bars
Rear suspension	Live axle, leaf springs
Axle ratio	2.93 or 3.31:1
Brakes, front/rear	Drum/drum

General

Wheelbase, in.	122
Height, in.	54.8
Width, in.	79.4
Length, in.	217
Weight, lb.	3,945

The recession of 1958 hurt DeSoto badly; sales hit a low of 49,445 units, which was 13,000 units less than Ford's jumbo failure, the Edsel. Adventurer production in 1958 was 350 hardtops and eighty-two convertibles.

Things continued to slide for DeSoto in 1959. Production was consolidated within the Chrysler Division's Jefferson Avenue plant, while DeSoto's plant at Warren, Michigan, was assigned to build Imperials. Sales, unfortunately, continued to decline to new lows.

Still, the 1959 Adventurer was a fine car. Color choice was either white or black, and the car shared in all the innovations of other 1959 Chrysler products: swivel front seats, automatic headlight dimmer and so on. The basic body shell was the same one as introduced in 1957. The Turboflash V-8 was enlarged to 383 ci and 350 hp, again with two four-barrel carburetors. Production of the Adventurer hardtop was only 590 units and only ninety-seven convertibles.

The year 1960 marked the last Adventurer. Now built as a unibody, it was available as a two-door hardtop, four-door sedan and four-door hardtop—and unfortunately

The 320 hp 341 ci Hemi engine was good for over 135 mph. *Larry Zappone*

the make lost the exclusivity it had enjoyed in the past. On the whole, the DeSoto line suffered degradation because only one other model besides the Adventurer was offered. Since it looked much like a Chrysler and cost almost as much, it helped to decide the DeSoto's fate, at least from the buying public's point of view. The 1961 DeSoto with its unusual two-tier grille nailed the coffin shut. There were plans for a 1962, but the prototype looked as if it had been styled by someone who had seen too many horror movies.

Prospects

The DeSoto Adventurer right now is in the sleeper category, as is the Pace car. From a historical perspective, these were the most luxurious and expensive, fastest and rarest of all DeSotos. Interestingly, these cars also have a poor survival rate, so few exist.

The 1957 DeSoto Adventurer embodied all the elements of Exner's Forward Look, while retaining the Adventurer's distinctive glittery look. *Alan Linsky*

The 1958 Adventurer featured revised side-spear paint which gave the car a lighter, sleeker look. This is one of the few convertibles still in existence. *Jim DeGregorio*

For 1959, the Adventurer available only in white
or black featured a restyled grille. *Galen Erb*

All Adventurers came with front swivel seats.
Galen Erb

Dual four-barrel 383 wedge was standard equipment. *Galen Erb*

The 1960 Adventurer was no longer the high-performance specialty automobile it once was, yet it was still distinctive. This is Alan Orenstein's pristine restoration.

These interesting swivel seats never really
caught on.

Chapter 6

1955–83 Imperial

★★★	1955-56 Imperial
★★★	1957-63 Imperial
★★★★	1957-63 Imperial Crown convertible
★★★★	1957-65 Ghia limousine
★★★	1964-68 Imperial
★★★↲	1964-68 Imperial Crown convertible
★★★↲	1967-70 Stageway Imperial limousine
★★	1969-75 Imperial
★★	1981-83 Imperial

Until 1955, the Imperial name was used to label the most luxurious models in the Chrysler line. In the late 1920s and early 1930s, this meant something, but during the Depression, Chrysler gradually abandoned the upper end of the market, building only a small number of limousines and long-wheelbase sedans under the Custom Imperial and, later, Crown Imperial label. This situation did not change after World War II—for example, production for 1946, 1947 and 1948 totaled 1,400 limousines and eight-passenger sedans. These were large and heavy automobiles, weighing over 4,800 lb. and built on a 145.5 inch wheelbase. Production in 1949 hit a low point: a mere eighty-five were built, followed by a slightly better year in 1950 when 415 units were produced.

In 1951, however, the Chrysler Imperial expanded to a four model series. Under the Crown Imperial banner, the limousine and eight-passenger sedan continued to be available, again ever so modestly at 700 units. Under the Imperial label, a four-door sedan, hardtop, club coupe and convertible were available. These were based on the New Yorker 131.5 inch wheelbase and, in fact, used the New Yorker body shell. All were powered by the new FirePower 331 ci Hemi. Sales from 1951 to 1954 totaled 42,480—considerably more. Yet the Imperial suffered from too close identification with other Chryslers: lack of a fully automatic transmission (rectified by June 1953 with the availability of the two-speed PowerFlite) and generally poor styling.

If Chrysler was serious about the luxury market, obviously some changes had to be made. The luxury market since the late 1930s was totally dominated by Cadillac. Owning a Cadillac had always meant that you had arrived, that you were a success. Its

---

1955 Imperial

Engine
Type	V-8
Bore x stroke, in.	3.81 x 3.63
Displacement, cubic in.	331
Compression ratio	8.5:1
Horsepower	250@4600
Torque	340@2800

Chassis and drivetrain
Transmission	2-spd automatic
Front suspension	Independent, coil springs
Rear suspension	Live axle, leaf springs
Axle ratio	NA
Brakes, front/rear	Drum/drum

General
Wheelbase, in.	130
Height, in.	61.2 (loaded)
Width, in.	79.1
Length, in.	223
Weight, lb.	4,565

Restyled 1955 Imperial brought the marque into
the fifties. Especially handsome is the two-door
version. *John Maclay*

1956 Imperial	
Engine	
Type	V-8
Bore x stroke, in.	3.94 x 3.63
Displacement, cubic in.	354
Compression ratio	9.0:1
Horsepower	280@4600
Torque	370@2800
Chassis and drivetrain	
Transmission	2-spd automatic
(3-spd automatic late 1956)	
Front suspension	Independent, coil springs
Rear suspension	Live axle, leaf springs
Brakes, front/rear	Drum/drum
General	
Wheelbase, in.	130
Height, in.	61.2
Width, in.	79.1
Length, in.	223
Weight, lb.	4,565

styling (at times incredible) had been responsible: Cadillacs were large, luxurious, powerful and blatant. Owning a Cadillac, however, did not mean that you had class. Part of the reason that Cadillac is no longer the car to own is because Cadillac went for volume. Too many people owned them, and somehow the downsized Cadillacs never seemed to convey the same feeling of opulence, luxury and exclusivity.

1955-56 Imperial

Part of the problem for Chrysler was that the name Imperial was not well known by the public, and it was always the "Chrysler" Imperial. In 1955, Imperial was set up as a separate division of Chrysler, a change that also coincided with new, fresh styling for the cars. Two models were offered: an Imperial four-door sedan and a Newport two-door hardtop, which bore a great resemblance to the C300. A 250 hp version of the 331 ci Hemi powered the Imperial. Other standard features included the PowerFlite automatic, power steering, brakes, windows and four-way seat. Under the Crown Imperial name, the limousine and eight-passenger sedan were offered, now built on a 149.5 inch wheelbase. These were big cars.

Even though Imperial production doubled, it is obvious that the Chrysler C300, with its Imperial looks, stole much of Imperial's

Appealing to a more conservative buyer was the four-door sedan. *John Lloyd*

thunder in 1955. The C300 with its winning race record and high performance was the most talked-about car in 1955. Perhaps the C300 should have been an Imperial. That would have given the Imperial a tremendous boost.

The year 1956 saw a slightly restyled Imperial as the Forward Look evolved. This was most evident in the finned rear fenders.

All Imperials used a 280 hp version of the 354 ci Hemi mated to the two-speed Power-Flite automatic—until midmodel year when the superior three-speed TorqueFlite made its appearance. The electrical system was improved by changing to a twelve-volt system.

Model line-up included the Imperial four-door sedan, while under the Southhampton

The 1956 Imperial grille remained the same. However, like the other Chrysler products, the rear end got these moderate fins. This is a two-door Southampton coupe.

The last year for the Crown Imperial limousine was 1956. From 1957 on, Imperial limousines would be built by Ghia. *Bob McVoy*

name, two-door and four-door hardtops replaced the Newport. All were built on a 133 inch wheelbase.

The last year for the Crown Imperial limousine and eight-passenger sedans built by Chrysler in the United States was 1956. These were similar to the 1955 versions built on a 149.5 inch wheelbase but were powered by the 280 hp engine. Production was a low 226 units.

A 1957 Imperial Southampton four-door. Styling was totally different from earlier Imperials. *Chrysler Corporation*

Prospects

The 1955–56 Imperials are important from a historical point of view and are an excellent embodiment of Exner's Forward Look. Look only for modest appreciation with these relatively plentiful cars. The two-door models are leading the way, with the 1956 Southampton getting the nod over a 1955 Newport because of better electrics and styling.

1957-63 Imperial

Chrysler Corporation's forte has always been engineering leadership. Power steering, alternators, hydraulic brakes and electronic ignition are only some of the engineering features that Chrysler made practical for mass-produced automobiles. Generally Chrysler played it safe by building conservative-looking cars and, at best, followed the styling themes set by the industry's leader, General Motors. Only once in the post-World War II period has Chrysler fielded a complete line of uniquely expressive cars that wrestled styling leadership

from GM, and that was 1957. Unfortunately, Chrysler was unable to follow up, and styling in the early 1960s took a dive.

The Imperial for 1957 had its own body with curved side glass, a first in an American

This is the 1957 Crown convertible. Note small crowns over headlights and the optional Continental spare trunk. This particular car was originally owned by Howard Hughes. *Paul J. Connolly*

83

The 1958s were slightly restyled. Quad headlights were standard equipment. This rear view
shows standard trunk. *Chrysler Corporation*

This is a 1958 LeBaron four-door sedan. *Chrysler Corporation*

production car. Three separate series were available: the Imperial (four-door hardtop, four-door sedan and two-door hardtop), the Imperial Crown (four-door hardtop, four-door sedan, two-door hardtop and convertible) and the Imperial LeBaron (four-door sedan and four-door hardtop). LeBaron had been a small coachbuilder of custom-made bodies during the 1920s and 1930s but was later absorbed by the Briggs Manufacturing Company which built bodies for Chrysler. Chrysler used the LeBaron name after it bought out Briggs to designate the top-of-the-line Imperial. The name Southhampton was also used on all hardtops.

The Crown series could be differentiated from the standard Imperial by a small gold crown dotting the second "i" in the name Imperial and by two gold crowns over each headlight brow. The LeBaron replaced the Imperial fender script with a medallion and

also used special wheel covers. The LeBaron also was available only in solid colors with interiors finished in a wool broadcloth.

The Flite Sweep Deck Lid, the official name for the Continental spare and trunk treatment, was optional on all Imperials. Dual headlights were optional as well in states where the lights were approved (at extra cost on the standard Imperial). The Highway Hi-Fi option, first seen in 1956, continued to be available. It played seven-inch records at $16\frac{2}{3}$ rpm and, as you'd expect, not very well.

Like the rest of Chrysler's offerings, the Imperial was equipped with the new front torsion bar suspension and also benefited from the standard TorqueFlite automatic. The engine, now enlarged to 392 ci, put out 325 hp from a single four-barrel carburetor.

For cost reasons, the limousines were now built by Ghia of Turin, Italy. Imperial South-

A 1958 Crown hardtop. *Chrysler Corporation*

hampton coupes were shipped to Ghia where the wheelbase was extended to 149.5 inches. These were virtually custom-built and extremely luxurious. A total of thirty-two exterior and interior combinations were available. Interiors were finished in either beige or gray with matching sheared mouton carpeting and the finest glove leather; rich woods and hand-crafted metals were used to trim the interior. All thirty-six pro-duced in 1957 used 1958 grilles, and this happened to be the highest number produced in a single year until production stopped in 1965.

The year 1958 saw minor trim changes. The 392 ci Hemi, now rated at 345 hp, powered the Imperial. But the 1958 recession saw sales drop by over fifty percent from 1957, whereas Cadillac sales dropped by less than fifteen percent. It takes time to

Swivel seats found their way into the 1959 Imperial.

1957 Imperial

Engine

Type	V-8
Bore x stroke, in.	4.00 x 3.90
Displacement, cubic in.	392
Compression ratio	9.25:1
Horsepower	325@4600
Torque	NA

Chassis and drivetrain

Transmission	3-spd automatic
Front suspension	Independent, torsion bars
Rear suspension	Live axle, leaf springs
Axle ratio	3.18:1
Brakes, front/rear	Drum/drum

General

Wheelbase, in.	129
Height, in.	57.5
Width, in.	81.2
Length, in.	224
Weight, lb.	4,640-4,780

The 1959 Imperial hardtop with its toothy grille.
Richard Matson

establish a name and image, and clearly Imperial had not been able to do so. In fact, Imperial never did, because production never exceeded the 1957 high of 37,557 units. Until Chrysler stopped production in 1975, only twice did sales break the 20,000 barrier, in 1964 and 1969, both times when a new body style was introduced. Cadillac, on the other hand, was selling over 200,000 units per year from 1967 on.

Changes on the 1959 version included a toothier front grille and the replacement of the Hemi with a 413 wedge rated at 350 hp. The entry-level Imperial was now called the Imperial Custom, a practice that continued until the 1964. A new option was the automatic self-leveling suspension to counter GM's similar system.

Chrysler did not have the resources for a complete restyle of the Imperial, particularly in the light of its low production. At a time when the public expected a complete restyle every few years, the Imperial by 1959 looked a little dated. In 1960, we saw a new "happy face" grille and more pronounced "batmobile" rear fins, but the basic shell was still the same. Sales, too, stabilized at around the 17,000 mark. Unlike the rest of Chrysler's offerings, the Imperial was the only line that did not switch to a unibody in 1960.

Exner, by this time, believed that the next breakthrough design would be similar to the styling found on his 1960 Valiant, which exhibited new, fresh, if not different, styling. The proportions were as correct as they could be, long hood and short deck, yet his interpretation of other classic 1930s elements was way off, particularly as applied on the bigger cars, and resulted in some unusual designs that, to put it mildly, were not well received. By 1961, Virgil Exner was replaced by Elwood Engel; however, Exner's styling influence was still in evidence until 1963.

Although the Imperial was not "Valiant-ized," the 1961 Imperial bore some new Exner styling features, most notably the free-standing headlights, which remained until the restyled Engel Imperial made its debut in 1964. The sedans were dropped so only two- and four-door hardtops were available, plus the convertible. The engine for the 1961–63 Imperial was still the 413 ranging from 350 hp in 1961 to 340 hp on the 1962–63 models.

Basically, these cars represented a holding action until the restyled Imperial of 1964 was ready. There is no question that by this time, the Imperial did look dated, especially when compared to the new Lincolns, re-

A 1958 Ghia limousine. *Walt VonDeppen*

The 1960 Imperial smiling grille. *Chrysler Corporation*

match the free-standing headlights, free-standing taillights, much like those found on the 1955–56 models, were used. The 1963 version was the recipient of a restyled grille, new taillights and a squared-off roof.

Prospects

The most desirable models of the 1957–63 Imperials are the relatively few convertibles that were built. They exemplify the flamboyance and excess that characterized the era. Parts are available, if you look hard enough. Rust is a problem, especially on the 1957–59 Imperials, but to a great degree, this depends on how the car was taken care of and in what part of the country it has spent its time. The rare Ghia limousines are desirable and interesting. Restoration, though, can be extremely difficult because so many parts were custom-made. The 1957–63 Imperials are also known as great demolition derby cars because of their remarkable inherent strength. They could outlast anything. It is especially sad to hear that a few of the fabulous Ghia limousines ended up this way.

The two-door and four-door hardtops and sedans are more common and represent a

styled in 1961. Even Cadillac toned things down a bit after the overdone 1959–60 models.

For 1962, the Imperial was shorn of its rear fins, while the grille was restyled. To

The 1960 Imperial LeBaron looks big and heavy and it was, too. *Walt VonDeppen*

The ultimate Imperial—in terms of outlandish-ness—is the 1961. This was also the last hurrah for fins.

good buy. There is no point at this time in restoring a complete basket case. You are much better off getting a restored example because these will appreciate much more slowly than the convertibles or Ghias. The Imperial always had a good highway ride, unlike anything that is available today. A little updating, such as radial tires and good shock absorbers will make this unusual comfort even better.

1964-68 Imperial

After seven years of basically the same design, the Imperial completely broke with the past in 1964. It was a good change, and the man responsible was Elwood Engel who replaced Virgil Exner in 1962. Engel, who had worked for Ford previously, was responsible for the 1961 Lincoln and Thun-

To capture the "classic" look, 1961 Imperials came with free-standing headlights.

A 1961 Imperial convertible with the optional trunk lid. Dash design is bizarre by today's standards but it is visually interesting. The CB radio is owner installed. *Jack Parry*

The 1962, still with the free-standing headlights, came with a restyled grille, but without the fins.

Taillights were mounted a la 1955-56 Imperial. *David Totten*

The 1963 Imperial saw another grille variation with the unusual headlights.

1965 Imperial	
Engine	
Type	V-8
Bore x stroke, in.	4.19 x 3.75
Displacement, cubic in.	413
Compression ratio	10.1:1
Horsepower	360@4800
Torque	470@3200
Chassis and drivetrain	
Transmission	3-spd automatic
Front suspension	Independent, torsion bars
Rear suspension	Live axle, leaf springs
Axle ratio	2.93:1
Brakes, front/rear	Drum/drum
General	
Wheelbase, in.	129
Height, in.	56.8
Width, in.	80.0
Length, in.	227.8
Weight, lb.	5,380
Performance	
0-60 mph	11.1
¼-mile e.t.@mph	19@75
Source	*Motor Trend, 7/1965*

1967 Imperial	
Engine	
Type	V-8
Bore x stroke, in.	4.32 x 3.75
Displacement, cubic in.	440
Compression ratio	10.1:1
Horsepower	350@4400
Torque	480@2800
Chassis and drivetrain	
Transmission	3-spd automatic
Front suspension	Independent, torsion bars
Rear suspension	Live axle, leaf springs
Axle ratio	2.94:1
Brakes, front/rear	Disc/drum
General	
Wheelbase, in.	127
Height, in.	56.2
Width, in.	79.6
Length, in.	224.7
Weight, lb.	5,230
Performance	
0-60 mph	9.6
¼-mile e.t.@mph	17.4@82.8
Source	*Car Life, 1/1967*

derbird. Thus the 1964 bore a great resemblance to the Lincoln, and in that sense, the 1964 and later Imperials were derivative rather than revolutionary, reflecting a conservative corporate policy that preferred to follow accepted design rather than to set precedents.

Whereas earlier Imperials had smooth, curved surfaces, the 1964 was flat and angular, almost boxy. The front used a split grille

A 1963 LeBaron Southampton four-door. *Tom Smith*

Free-standing taillights were dropped in favor of this cleaner-looking taillight arrangement. *Chrysler Corporation*

while the distinctive rear bulged, simulating the look of the Continental spare. It was a simple, yet distinctive design.

Mechanically, the 1964 Imperial was almost unchanged from the 1963. The big 413 engine was used with the three-speed TorqueFlite automatic, which still had push-button controls. Engine output was 340 hp.

Two models were offered: the Imperial Crown in two-door and four-door hardtop and convertible configurations and the Imperial LeBaron only as a four-door hardtop. One way to tell the Crown from the Le-Baron was that the LeBaron used a much smaller rear window. The Imperials continued to be built on a 129 inch wheelbase

Rare 1963 Ghia limousine. *Chrysler Corporation*

The Engel-styled 1964s brought the Imperial into the 1960s. Side view resemblance to 1961 Lincoln is very pronounced, yet the rear-end treatment and grille are unique. This is a rare Crown convertible. *Walt VonDeppen*

A 1965 Imperial with its glass-covered head-lights. This is the Crown coupe. *Chrysler Corporation*

with front torsion bar suspension and leaves at the rear. Power steering and power brakes with drums all around were also standard equipment.

Sales improved considerably, reaching 23,285—still small potatoes when compared to Cadillac (165,959), but a lot closer to Lincoln (36,297).

The year 1965 marked the end of the Ghia limousines. This is one of ten built. *Walt VonDeppen*

Some consider the 1966 Imperial to be the last true Imperial. It was still built the old-fashioned way (body-on-frame) and it did not share its body with any other Chrysler product. In any case, the 1964–66 Imperials are the best bet for appreciation. *Chrysler Corporation*

The 1965 version saw minor changes. The grille was restyled with headlights grouped behind tempered glass panels, which resembled the Chrysler 300 grille. The interiors featured trim changes.

The 1966 was restyled slightly, with a different front grille. The biggest change was the use of the new 440 ci engine, a bored-out 413, rated at 350 hp.

Sales unfortunately declined to 13,743 by 1966. The car was more luxurious than ever, yet it could not get the acceptance needed to make it a marketing success.

Styling on the 1967–68 Imperials was similar to that of the 1964–66s: angular and slab-sided. There were important beneath-the-skin differences, however. For cost reasons, the Imperial was now based on the Chrysler unibody shell. Even though the resemblance to other Chryslers was greater than ever, the Imperial still managed to have a luxurious, Imperial feel to it.

The drivetrain was the same as that found on the 1966 Imperial, the 350 hp 440 with the TorqueFlite automatic. Front disc brakes became standard with the 1967 Imperial, and the line-up was the same as before, although a four-door sedan version was added to the Crown Series.

Ghia limousine production ended with the 1965 model, with only ten 1964s and ten 1965s built. An additional ten limousines were built in 1966 after the tooling was moved to Spain. Thereafter Imperial limousines were built by Stageway of Fort Smith,

A rare and unique option in 1966 (only 44 made) was the Mobile Director Option. The conference table, when not in use, tucked in between the rear seat. Front-passenger seat swiveled 180 degrees to create a conference room on wheels.

Arkansas, a domestic manufacturer who specialized in stretched versions of standard sedans and wagons. The Stageway Imperials were built on a very long 163 inch wheelbase and measured 260 inches in length. Production stopped in 1970.

Prospects

Taken as a group, the 1964–68 Imperials are the most desirable of any Imperials, but these remain reasonably priced. The convertibles are still in the sleeper category and should eventually catch on. The styling is

Although the 1967 Imperial shared the New Yorker's body shell, it still had enough individuality to stand on its own. *Chrysler Corporation*

unquestionably classic. As with most Chryslers, parts availability is not the greatest, and you are better off purchasing a restored example.

1969–83 Imperial

The 1969–73 Imperial looked more like a dressed-up Chrysler than the separate entity it once was. The styling for 1969 was new, featuring bulging, rounded sides and was termed fuselage styling (fuselarge) by Chrysler. In spite of the fact that the Imperial was a luxurious automobile, it was no longer a contender in the luxury field.

Mechanically, it was similar to its predecessors. Built on a 127 inch wheelbase, the 350 hp 440 ci V-8 coupled to the TorqueFlite automatic was the only drivetrain combination available. Power steering, brakes and windows were all standard equipment.

By 1971, Imperial was no longer a separate Chrysler division, and availability was limited to only LeBaron two-door and four-door hardtops. On the engineering front, a Bendix four-wheel anti-skid braking system was optionally available. It never caught on, and although it was not as sophisticated as today's ABS systems, it worked well enough.

In 1974 Chrysler redesigned the Imperial; this time it shared the 124 inch platform with the New Yorker. Styling was derivative, featuring the Lincoln Mark IV look. But by 1975, what did the car in was the first oil crisis. Huge cars were just not as acceptable as they once were.

On June 12, 1975, after 8,830 units, production was halted because of poor sales.

The Imperial made a brief comeback during 1981, 1982 and 1983, this time based on the Cordoba and Mirada. Strictly conventional in design, it looked like a Lincoln arriving and a Cadillac Seville departing. It was powered by a fuel-injected 318 V-8 that proved to be unreliable. The front suspension used a transverse torsion bar while the rear used a live axle on leaf springs, just like

A 1967 convertible. *Chrysler Corporation*

The 1968 Imperial got a restyled grille and rear-end treatment. The convertible is particularly attractive and it is also the last year it was available.

the 1955 Imperial! It actually wasn't a bad car, but timing was off because the industry and the nation's economy were going through one of the worst recessions since World War II. The car didn't catch on, and production stopped with the 1983 model after a three-year production run of 12,385 units.

Prospects

The 1969 and later Imperials have little collector value with little prospect for appreciation. They do have a nice ride in the traditional sense, and if you've always wanted a big—really big—car, the Imperial is hard to beat.

A 1969 Imperial with its rounded, fuselage styling. Resemblance to the New Yorker was strong. *Chrysler Corporation*

Styling through 1973 consisted of restyled grilles and tails on the same basic body shell. This is a 1971.

A 1973 Chrysler Imperial LeBaron four-door hardtop. *Chrysler Corporation*

The last restyle occurred in 1974. *Chrysler Corporation*

Dismal sales finally forced Chrysler to withdraw the Imperial in 1975, thereby giving up the high end of the market. This is a LeBaron coupe.

Distinctive grille has been dubbed the "waterfall" grille.

Chrysler reintroduced the Imperial in 1981. A good-looking car, it failed to attract enough buyers. It has little collector value. *Chrysler Corporation*

Chapter 7

The Fabulous Bs

★★	1966-70 Dodge Coronet
★★★	1967-70 Coronet R/T
★★★	1968-71 Dodge Super Bee
★★★	1966-71 Plymouth Belvedere, GTX
★★★	1968-72 Plymouth Road Runner
★★★	1972-74 Road Runner
★★★★	1969-70 Belvedere and Road Runner convertibles
★★★★★	1970 Plymouth Super Bird
★★	1966-67 Dodge Charger
★★★	1968-70 Charger
★★	1971-74 Charger
★★★★★	1969 Charger 500 and Charger Daytona
★★★★	With 440 six-barrel
★★★★★	With 426 Hemi

When you think of a Chrysler muscle car, the picture that comes to mind is that of a big, rumbling intermediate, whether it is a GTX, Charger, Super Bee or Road Runner. These were tough, street terrors that relied on simplicity (as far as styling goes) and cubic inches to establish their street supremacy. Sure, GM and Ford had their hot runners, but it was the Chrysler supercars that ran well and reliably, even with the base engine that in most cases was a four-barrel 383. To get a comparable Ford to perform, you had to buy the top engine option, usually a 428CJ, and then you had to play with it to get it to run. GM had the popular GTO, but how secure would you feel with an engine that came with a cast-iron crank, cast rods and pistons?

The big Chrysler cars ran impressively well "out of the box"—you didn't have to do anything to them, and if you wanted massive overkill, there was always the awesome 426 Hemi. The Hemi-powered cars offered incredible acceleration—no other American

Dodge's intermediate was the Coronet. Restyled in 1966, it was available with the Hemi.

The 1967 Coronet used the same grille as the Dodge Charger, but without having hidden headlights.

103

production engine could match it. A Chevrolet enthusiast may say, what about the L-88 powered Corvette? True, it was a production car, but it was barely streetable and to discourage street use, L-88 powered cars did not even have a heater! Chrysler was committed to performance; from 1966 to 1971, about 11,000 Hemi-powered cars were built. No other manufacturer came close to producing that many street cars with what

was essentially a slightly detuned race engine.

Chrysler first used the 426 Hemi during the 1964 Daytona 500 stock car race. Although the 413 and 426 Max Wedge engines were doing well in drag racing, they were not as successful on the stock car racetracks. In 1961 and 1962, Pontiacs won the most races, and in 1963, Ford took the lead. Chrysler needed a strong race engine to

A 1968 Dodge Coronet R/T, Dodge's version of the Plymouth GTX. Using the same platform was the Dodge Super Bee, equivalent to but less popular than Plymouth's Road Runner. *Chrysler Corporation*

The 1969 Coronet R/T sported this rear taillight treatment. *Chrysler Corporation*

dominate the NASCAR tracks, which would help Chrysler's performance image in the marketplace.

Chrysler had experience with Hemi engines since 1951 when the 331 ci FirePower was introduced. The ultimate development of that engine, reached in 1957, displaced 392 ci. The FirePower-equipped Chrysler 300s easily swept the NASCAR circuit, but by 1958, Chrysler stopped producing the

Distinguishing features of the 1969 R/T included the rear stripe, dummy rear brake scoops and the functional hood which was standard with Hemi-powered R/Ts.

early Hemi, as it is now commonly referred to, for cost reasons.

Because there wasn't enough time to develop a new engine from the ground up, Chrysler basically applied the early Hemi's technology to the RB (raised block) 426 block. The stress-relieved block featured cross-bolted main bearing caps, and to ensure durability, every component was designed, built and tested for use only in the 426 Hemi. The Hemi-powered Plymouths easily won the 1964 Daytona 500, finishing one-two-three, and they managed to win twenty-six of the sixty-two Grand National NASCAR races that year. Still, Fords man-

Interior, like all the other B intermediates, was simple and functional with very slight emphasis on luxury. Additional gauges are owner installed.

High point for the Super Bee in 1969 was the availability of the 440 Six Pack.

aged to win thirty races because of better preparation and durability. Rule disputes kept the Hemi-powered cars out of racing for most of 1965. Rules for the 1966 season, though, made it difficult for Chrysler's and for Ford's sohc 427s—both limited-production engines—to race unless they were installed in regular production passenger cars. Chrysler felt that the advantages of winning on the racetrack outweighed the cost of producing street versions of the Hemi, and so from 1966, the street Hemi was available on Dodge and Plymouth cars.

The street Hemi did not differ too drastically from race versions. It used a milder solid lifter camshaft, lower 10.25:1 compression ratio, an aluminum inline dual-plane intake manifold with two Carter four-barrel carburetors and cast-iron exhaust manifolds. It was rated at 425 hp at 5000 rpm with 490 lb-ft of torque at 4000 rpm. These specifications remained unchanged until 1971, the last year the engine was available, even though cam specs were changed in 1968 (slightly longer duration and overlap). Hy-draulic lifters were used on engines from 1970 on.

Production stopped in 1971 for the well-known reason that high insurance premiums made the engine too costly, but also because NASCAR changed rules once again, limiting engine size to 305 ci.

Obviously, the Hemi-powered 1966–71 intermediates using the B-body platform

The 1970 Super Bee and its odd styling.

and the 1970–71 Barracuda and Challenger E-body pony cars are the most desirable of all Chrysler-produced cars of the 1960s and early 1970s. It is critical that you know how to identify these monsters; here are some important things to know and look for.

All Hemi cars used a convertible body with a roof section attached to it. The reason for this was that the convertible body was stronger than the regular hardtop. The con-

Odd styling or not, the mere fact that this 1970 Super Bee has the 426 Hemi makes it an instant collectible.

vertible also had torque boxes that connected the rear bulkhead into the siderails in front of each rear leaf spring. This not only stiffened the chassis but also serves as a means of identifying a Hemi car. These boxes can be seen if you take a look underneath. All four-speed cars came with the Dana 60 rear, and none were available with air conditioning.

All Hemi cars came with a thick steel plate welded to the floor of the car above the rear pinion snubber, and all came with a ⅜ inch interior dimension fuel line (as did 440 powered cars). Standard fuel line interior dimension was ⁵⁄₁₆ inch.

Hemi-powered cars also had a different K-frame that was used to mount the engine. They all came with the large radiator support and large radiator used in air conditioned cars; all automatics came with an auxiliary transmission oil cooler, and all cars (with the exception of the 1971 B-bodies) came with a side-mounted windshield wiper motor to provide clearance for the air cleaner or fresh air scoop. All 1969 and later Hemi cars (except for the Super Bird, Charger Daytona and 1970 Charger) came with outside air induction as standard equipment. Cars from 1968 and earlier did not, except for the factory racers.

A 1966 Plymouth Belvedere I with the 426 Hemi. Lower fender emblem is the only giveaway that this is not an unmarked police car.

I admit that I have found all the variations of the B-bodies initially confusing as they all—except the Dodge Charger—look alike.

1966-71 Dodge Coronet, Coronet R/T and Super Bee

Although the Coronet was first introduced in 1965 as Dodge Division's entry in the intermediate-size field, it was successfully restyled in 1966. For the enthusiast, of interest was the availability of the 426 street Hemi in the two-door model, but according to Galen Govier, at least two four-door sedans are known to exist. You really had to look hard to tell whether a Coronet came with the Hemi or not. The car was fast, but lacked any performance image.

The 1967 Coronet featured a slight grille and taillight change, but of more importance was the introduction of a new model specifically with performance in mind. This was the Coronet R/T (road and track). Standard

1968 Dodge R/T convertible	
Engine	
Type	V-8
Bore x stroke, in.	4.32 x 3.75
Displacement, cubic in.	440
Compression ratio	10.0:1
Horsepower	375@4600
Torque	480@3200
Optional engine	426 Hemi
Chassis and drivetrain	
Transmission	3-spd automatic
Optional transmission	4-spd manual
Front suspension	Independent, torsion bars
Rear suspension	Live axle, leaf springs
Axle ratio	3.23:1
Brakes, front/rear	Disc/drum
General	
Wheelbase, in.	117
Height, in.	52.5
Width, in.	76.7
Length, in.	206.6
Weight, lb.	3,845
Performance	
0-60 mph	6.6
¼-mile e.t.@mph	14.69@97.4
Source	Car Life, 4/1968

The 1967 Belvedere GTX at a quick glance looks like a typical family sedan.

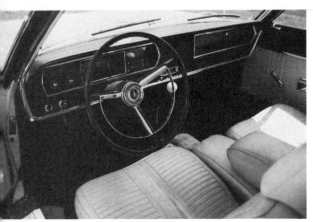

The interior, too, is on the plain side.

engine was the husky 440 four-barrel, dubbed Magnum, putting out 375 hp and 480 lb-ft of torque. Standard equipment included bucket seats, console with floor shifter, heavy-duty suspension, larger drum brakes, the three-speed TorqueFlite automatic and simulated hood scoops. Optional were power disc brakes, four-speed manual transmission and, of course, the 426 Hemi. The R/T grille resembled the one that came with the Charger, but the lights were not retractable. Side stripes and appropriate R/T identification set the car off, although these items could be deleted.

You could order the R/T, and the rest of the Coronet line, with a host of other comfort and trim options. Sales totaled 10,181 units, which included 628 convertibles. Only 283 Hemi-powered R/Ts were built.

The Coronet got restyled for the better in 1968. Mechanically, the R/T remained the same, but to set off the styling, Chrysler offered either side stripes or the new bumblebee stripes that were wrapped around the tail. The bumblebee stripes became the trademark of the Scat Pack, a grouping of the Dodge high-performance models, which

The King—425 hp 426 Hemi.

included the Charger R/T, Coronet R/T and Dart GTS. Around mid-1968, Dodge announced the introduction of the Super Bee to coincide with Plymouth's Road Runner.

The Super Bee was based on the Coronet 440 two-door coupe that used pop-out rear windows. Because it was intended as an econo street racer, it featured minimal trim but did include the power bulge hood from the Coronet R/T and the instrument panel from the Charger.

Standard engine was the 335 hp version of the 383 which used many parts from the 375 hp 440 engine, such as the cylinder heads with their larger exhaust valves of 1.74 inches versus 1.60 inches, camshaft, exhaust manifolds and windage tray. The engine was connected to an efficient 2¼ inch dual exhaust system. Standard transmission was a four-speed manual, with the three-speed TorqueFlite automatic optional. Drum brakes were standard, but power discs were optional. With the disc brakes you also got fifteen-inch wheels and tires rather than the

Optional chrome Magnum wheels do give the Belvedere a sportier look.

stock fourteen-inch rims. The Hemi was optional.

The year 1969 saw few changes. A single bumblebee stripe was used on both the

Rare 1968 GTX convertible. Convertibles, even without the Hemi, can command very high prices.

The 1968 GTX convertible interior. Note tachometer on the right part of the instrument panel.

1969 Dodge Super Bee

Engine
Type	V-8
Bore x stroke, in.	4.25 x 3.38
Displacement, cubic in.	383
Compression ratio	10.0:1
Horsepower	335@5200
Torque	425@3400

Chassis and drivetrain
Transmission	3-spd automatic
Front suspension	Independent, torsion bars
Rear suspension	Live axle, leaf springs
Axle ratio	3.55:1
Brakes, front/rear	Disc/drum

General
Wheelbase, in.	117
Height, in.	54.1
Width, in.	76.7
Length, in.	206.6
Weight, lb.	3,765

Performance
0–60 mph	5.6
¼-mile e.t.@mph	14.04@99.55
Source	*Car and Driver*, 1/1969

This is typical of a correctly restored engine and engine compartment. It belongs to a GTX convertible.

Super Bee and R/T. You could also get bucket seats with the Super Bee; bench seats were standard. Other visual changes were the optional rear-quarter-panel scoops and the optional Ramcharger fresh air induction hood that used two functional hood scoops. This hood became standard equipment on Hemi-equipped R/Ts. Also, the Super Bee was available as a hardtop.

The biggest development in 1969 was the availability of the 440 Six Pack motor on the Super Bee. This was as close as you could get to Hemi-type acceleration for less money. In fact, on the street the 440 Six Pack could out-accelerate the Hemi to about 70 mph when the Hemi's superior breathing took over.

This was strictly a package that appealed to the street and strip set. Immediately noticeable was the flat black fiberglass hood held in place by four hood pins. Wheels were plain steel highlighted only by five chrome lugs. The G70x15 Goodyear Polyglas tires, the only ones available, just weren't enough to handle all that torque, however.

The 440 Six Pack used three two-barrel Holley carburetors mounted on an Edel-brock manifold, flowing 1350 cfm. Impressive to behold, all this carburetion airflow was a little too much for a street engine. The Super Bee came with either a four-speed manual or a TorqueFlite automatic, and used what was the strongest rear available in a street car, the Dana 60 with 4.10:1 ratio. As usual, drum brakes were standard equipment, with discs optional.

The final year for the Coronet R/T and Super Bee was 1970. The biggest change was the new dual loop grille that had an alien, not-from-this-planet look to it. The rear quarters were slightly restyled and used non-functional side scoops. To distinguish the R/T from the Super Bee, different taillights were used.

Engine line-up expanded on the R/T in 1970. The 375 hp 440 was standard, with the 440 Six Pack engine and 426 Hemi optional. The Six Pack engine used a Chrysler cast-iron manifold rather than the Edelbrock unit to save a few dollars.

The Super Bee was still promoted as a budget supercar with the 383 as standard equipment. The 440 Six Pack and 426 Hemi were optional. Standard transmission was

The 1968 Road Runner reflected the no-frills approach to muscle cars. The standard 383 provided excellent street performance, but for those who wanted more, the Hemi was available as an option. This Road Runner is one of the few that were ordered this way.

The 1969 GTX got a slightly restyled grille and graphics. Of course, Hemi-equipped examples are rare and desirable.

now a three-speed manual, but the four-speed manual and TorqueFlite automatic were optional. This year, however, the Six Pack engine did not come with a fiberglass hood. The Super Bee buyer also had a choice of two stripe treatments, the familiar wrap-around tail stripe or a new C-pillar rear-quarter stripe treatment. Other interesting options included a rear deck spoiler, the Tuff

Almost as potent as the Hemi was the 440 Six Pack Road Runner of 1969. Fiberglass hood and scoop have to be lifted off as a unit to expose the 440. This car has nonstock wheels.

114

steering wheel and hood-mounted tachometer.

Prospects

These cars, along with their Plymouth counterparts, represented what the Chrysler supercar of the 1960s was all about. The primary focus was on the lower end of the market in terms of cost, but they sure did go. The Six Pack and Hemi cars are rare and desirable, especially the convertibles, but the other models can provide an excellent way for the enthusiast to participate in the 1960s supercar phenomenon.

Because of the way these cars were built and marketed, it is possible to find Super Bees and R/Ts without power steering, power brakes, air conditioning and even a radio—just a big engine. You are better off getting the most heavily optioned car you can find, which will be more enjoyable to drive and more valuable as well.

For 1969, the Road Runner interior was still simple, though this example has the optional bucket seats.

Engine and drive parts are available, but as with other unibody-designed cars, avoid rustbuckets. There is also little doubt that most of these cars were driven hard, modi-

The 440 Six Pack. This one has owner-installed exhaust headers.

The 1970 GTX looks meaner. Note Air Grabber hood. All GTXs came with simulated rear fender scoops. This is a 440 Six Pack.

fied and quite likely abused. Be careful, and make sure that you take a look at the under-carriage of the car that you are interested in. Bent and welded frames, and cracks at the spring mounts are not good signs. These cars are definitely not the type grandpa would buy and drive only on Sunday.

1966-71 Plymouth Belvederes, Belvedere GTXs and Road Runners

The Belvedere and its GTX and Road Runner offshoots were Plymouth's versions of the performance intermediates, equivalent to the Dodge Coronet, Coronet R/T and Super Bee. Although similar in styling to

A 1970 Road Runner with its standard 383. Stripe on hood is non-stock.

Decals graced the Road Runner's air cleaners,
in keeping with the cartoon character theme of a
hapless coyote chasing the Road Runner.

1967 Plymouth GTX	
Engine	
Type	V-8
Bore x stroke, in.	4.32 x 3.75
Displacement, cubic in.	440
Compression ratio	10.1:1
Horsepower	375@4600
Torque	480@3200
Chassis and drivetrain	
Transmission	3-spd automatic
Front suspension	Independent, torsion bars
Rear suspension	Live axle, leaf springs
Axle ratio	3.23:1
Brakes, front/rear	Disc/drum
General	
Wheelbase, in.	116
Height, in.	54
Width, in.	76.4
Length, in.	200.5
Weight, lb.	3,830
Performance	
0-60 mph	6.6
¼-mile e.t.@mph	15.2@97
Source	*Car Life*, 3/1967

1969 Plymouth Road Runner	
Engine	
Type	V-8
Bore x stroke, in.	4.25 x 3.38
Displacement, cubic in.	383
Compression ratio	10.0:1
Horsepower	335@5200
Torque	425@3200
Chassis and drivetrain	
Transmission	4-spd manual
Front suspension	Independent, torsion bars
Rear suspension	Live axle, leaf springs
Axle ratio	3.90:1
Brakes, front/rear	Drum/drum
General	
Wheelbase, in.	116
Height, in.	53.1
Width, in.	76.4
Length, in.	202.7
Weight, lb.	3,645
Performance	
0-60 mph	5.1
¼-mile e.t.@mph	14.7@100.6
Source	*Car Life*, 1/1969

their Dodge counterparts, the Plymouths outsold them by a large margin. The 426 Hemi engine was first available in 1966 on the Belvedere and the more deluxe Satellite, and as such, is by far more desirable than any other 1966 Plymouth. Powerful and expensive, not many of these were sold.

The year 1967 saw the introduction of the Belvedere GTX, with its standard 375 hp 440 four-barrel Super Commando engine.

Rarest of all Road Runners is the Road Runner Super Bird. Special nose cone and high rear wing drastically altered the car's appearance.

As with the Coronet R/T, the Hemi was optional. The GTX provided a performance image, but because it was based on the top-of-the-line model, sales were limited.

Plymouth enthusiasts were excited about the 1968 introduction of the Road Runner. Like the Super Bee, the Road Runner, which used the Road Runner cartoon character as its moniker, was the budget package designed to crush the competition on the street while being easily affordable. With a price of $2,869, it was a great straightline performance car with no frills. The Road Runner was based on the bottom-of-the-line Belvedere coupe with swing-out rear windows. A midyear introduction was a hardtop that also came with a higher level trim than the coupe. A Custom Decor Package was also available.

Even with the standard 335 hp 383, the Road Runner provided mid-fourteen-second (or better) quarter-mile times. It was a single-purpose machine and well equipped to perform the job it was designed for, with heavy-duty suspension, bigger brakes and stronger driveline than the regular Belvederes. A four-speed manual was included with the 383, while the TorqueFlite automatic was optional. Other options included power disc brakes with the fifteen-inch wheels, which from today's perspective are a necessity. Of course, the Hemi was optional.

1971 Plymouth GTX	
Engine	
Type	V-8
Bore x stroke, in.	4.31 x 3.75
Displacement, cubic in.	440
Compression ratio	9.7:1
Horsepower	370@4600
Torque	480@3200
Chassis and drivetrain	
Transmission	3-spd automatic
Front suspension	Independent, torsion bars
Rear suspension	Live axle, leaf springs
Axle ratio	3.23:1
Brakes, front/rear	Disc/drum
General	
Wheelbase, in.	115
Height, in.	53
Width, in.	79.1
Length, in.	203.2
Weight, lb.	4,022
Performance	
0-60 mph	6.5
¼-mile e.t.@mph	14.9@95.4
Source	*Car and Driver*, 11/1970

The Road Runner proved to be a marketing success, with over 44,000 units sold.

Sales in 1969 proved to be even better, with over 80,000 units sold. Plymouth saw fit to add a convertible to the line-up, and by midyear the 440 Six Pack engine, which bridged the gap between the Hemi and the 383. And it was a complete package, with the wild black fiberglass hood and special (Hemi)

Rear-facing fender scoops were for tire clearance on the race versions.

Nose cone also housed the retractable headlights.

Interior was typical taxi cab Road Runner.

suspension and driveline. This was strictly a quarter-mile car, with its 4.10:1 Dana rear.

In fact, that's where the emphasis of Chrysler's muscle cars was. They were not the best handling cars, partly due to the late 1960s tire technology and mostly because Chrysler focused on drag and NASCAR racing. Fiberglass-belted tires may have been OK in 1969, but a modern, high-performance set of radials will do wonders—as will the installation of the biggest rear sway bar you can find.

If you need more detailed information on the Road Runner and GTX up to 1969, refer to the Coronet R/T and Super Bee discussed above.

The 1970 GTX and Road Runner were based on the restyled Belvedere and bore an evolutionary resemblance to their predecessors, unlike the Coronet R/T and Super Bee. At first glance, they did not seem too different from the 1969 models, yet aside from the roof, these were new cars. Most noticeable was the new front grille, which gave the car a more attractive and aggressive look. Other styling features included the simulated rear

This particular Super Bird is equipped with the potent 440 Six Pack.

fender brake scoops, hood bulge and new taillight panel treatment. The convertible, though, was dropped from the GTX line but was still available on the Road Runner.

To counter Dodge's Scat Pack, Plymouth formed the Rapid Transit System, which grouped Plymouth's performance cars and enabled them to be marketed as a group showing: performance was available at all levels.

The GTX's engine and transmission options remained unchanged, with the excep-

The 1971 Road Runner and GTX were totally restyled. This Road Runner has the rare Hemi option. Note rear window louvers, and wing.

Road Runner character is in the center of the front grille.

Air Grabber hood. Paint on this car is obviously non-stock.

tion of the addition of the 440 Six Pack as an option. The Six Pack engine did not come with a fiberglass hood. Fresh air could be had with the Air Grabber, optional on either 440, but standard on the Hemi.

A nice option that improved the GTX and Road Runner's appearance and performance was the availability of 15x7 Rallye wheels with F60x15 Goodyear tires. There is nothing like a good set of wheels and tires to enhance a car's performance image.

The Road Runner was still available as a two-door coupe, hardtop and convertible.

Optional G60x15 tires on the attractive Rally wheels complemented the car's image and performance capabilities.

Standard engine was the popular 383, which was still rated at 335 hp, although compression dropped to 9.5:1. For 1970, a Holley four-barrel replaced the Carter as well. In a cost-cutting move, standard transmission was a three-speed manual, but the four-speed manual and TorqueFlite automatic were optional.

The 440 Six Pack and Hemi were optional, but as in previous years, only a small percentage of cars were equipped with these engines. One interesting change on the 426 Hemi was the switch to a hydraulic cam for emission reasons. Still rated at 425 hp, the engine ran in a subtly different way when compared with the solid lifter version—the solid lifter version felt stronger.

The most interesting Road Runner in 1970 was the Super Bird, Plymouth's NASCAR homologation special. As with the earlier Charger Daytona, Plymouth had to build a certain number of these cars if they were to be raced on the NASCAR tracks. Unlike the Daytona where only 500 were required, NASCAR changed the rules for 1970, necessitating that at least 2,000 Super Birds had to be built.

The Dodge Charger had been Chrysler's mainstay in NASCAR racing in the late 1960s because of its inherently better aerodynamics. Plymouth had offered its own version of Daytona-type aerodynamics, but only the defection of Richard Petty to Ford convinced Plymouth that in order to win it would need a similar car. Basically, the Daytona's nose cone and rear-mounted wing were adapted to the Road Runner, but there were differences. The Super Bird had to use Dodge Coronet fenders that were more downsloping, and a special plug was also needed to correct a hood-to-nose cone mismatch. You'll also note that the Super Bird had a larger air inlet and the rear wing was larger and swept back a bit more.

Engine availability was the same as with the GTXs, as was transmission choice. Power steering, power disc brakes and fourteen-inch Rallye wheels were all standard equipment. The larger fifteen-inch Rallye wheels were optional.

The Super Bird was available in seven colors: Alpine White, Lime Light, Lemon

The last year for the 426 Hemi was 1971.

Twist, Blue Fire Metallic, Tor-Red, Vitamin C Orange and Corporation Blue. Black or white vinyl graced the interior. Reflecting the Road Runner's no-frills heritage, a bench seat was standard, though you could get bucket seats too.

The Super Bird was an incredible car in 1970 and is even more so today, especially when you consider its sheer size. Coupled with the 426 Hemi (135 built) and depending on axle ratio, 160 mph and more is possible.

The year 1971 proved to be the last hurrah for the GTX and Road Runner from a performance standpoint. It was the last year for the GTX, which continued to be available with the same engine line-up as before.

The 1972 Road Runner was essentially the same car, except for minor styling changes and graphics. *Chrysler Corporation*

The year 1973 brought a new grille on the Road Runner which remained unchanged for 1974.

This 1974 Road Runner has the optional 440 four-barrel engine.

1966 Plymouth Satellite

Engine

Type	V-8
Bore x stroke, in.	4.25 x 3.75
Displacement, cubic in.	426
Compression ratio	10.25:1
Horsepower	425@5000
Torque	490@4500

Chassis and drivetrain

Transmission	3-spd automatic
Front suspension	Independent, torsion bars
Rear suspension	Live axle, leaf springs
Axle ratio	3.23:1
Brakes, front/rear	Drum/drum

General

Wheelbase, in.	116
Height, in.	53.2
Width, in.	75.5
Length, in.	200.5
Weight, lb.	3,940

Performance

0-60 mph	7.1
¼-mile e.t.@mph	14.5@95
Source	*Car Life,* 7/1966

Optional wheel covers on the 1966 Charger.

Engine output was marginally less due to a slight compression reduction and, of course, was a lot less when measured under the net rating system.

The Satellite body in GTX and Road Runner trim looked more aggressive and muscular than ever. The fuselage look that made Chrysler's big cars look really big and heavy, looked just right for the intermediates.

The Road Runner was offered to the public with the trusty four-barrel 383 rated at 300 hp. The big 440 Six Pack and 426 Hemi were still optional, but in an effort to mollify the local happy-go-lucky insurance agent, the small-block 340 rated at 275 hp was made an option at midyear. It didn't help much, as sales continued to slide. Interesting options for 1971 included a rear deck spoiler and rear window louvers, much like the ones available on the Barracuda and Challenger.

The 1966-67 Dodge Charger was not a complete styling success, though it was more attractive than other full fastbacks of that era. This 1966 has the Hemi engine.

Dash is dominated by four instrument pods.

The 1968 Dodge Charger hit a high point in Chrysler styling. *Chrysler Corporation*

More of the same came in 1972. The standard engine was now a 400, while a 340 hp and a 280 hp 440 were optional. The grille was slightly restyled, and revised tape stripes were available. But all in all, even though the big guns were gone, at least the basic artillery pieces were still there for the hot-rodder to improve upon.

In 1973 and 1974, Chrysler departed further from the Road Runner's original concept: the standard engine was a two-barrel 318 rated at 170 hp. Still, the 340 (360 in 1974), 400 and 440 engines were available. The last true Road Runners featured a restyled nose (as Chrysler backed away from loop bumpers) and the usual revised tape stripe treatments to add some pizzaz.

The 1975 Road Runner was based on "The Small Fury." In 1976 there was the Road Runner Package and Road Runner Decor Group for the Volare, which continued until 1980.

Prospects

The most unique Road Runner was the Super Bird, and accordingly, restored examples can bring over $20,000, and even more with the 426 Hemi. You can still find typical beat-up, unrestored Super Birds, and as long as the nose cone, rear wing and other unique pieces are in good shape, restoration should not be too difficult.

The convertibles are of interest next, followed by the hardtops and coupes. A GTX is probably nicer to have because it is more luxurious than the typical bare bones Road Runner. If you are not into strict originality,

The 1969 Charger got a grille divider and different taillights. This is a Hemi-powered Charger R/T.

1966 Dodge Charger	
Engine	
Type	V-8
Bore x stroke, in.	4.25 x 3.38
Displacement, cubic in.	383
Compression ratio	10.0:1
Horsepower	325@4800
Torque	425@2800
Chassis and drivetrain	
Transmission	3-spd automatic
Front suspension	Independent, torsion bars
Rear suspension	Live axle, leaf springs
Axle ratio	3.23:1
Brakes, front/rear	Drum/drum
General	
Wheelbase, in.	117
Height, in.	54.3
Width, in.	75.3
Length, in.	203.6
Weight, lb.	3,650
Performance	
0-60 mph	7.8
¼-mile e.t.@mph	16.2@88
Source	*Car and Driver*, 2/1966

1968 Dodge Charger R/T	
Engine	
Type	V-8
Bore x stroke, in.	4.25 x 3.75
Displacement, cubic in.	426
Compression ratio	10.25:1
Horsepower	425@5000
Torque	490@4000
Chassis and drivetrain	
Transmission	3-spd automatic
Front suspension	Independent, torsion bars
Rear suspension	Live axle, leaf springs
Axle ratio	3.23:1
Brakes, front/rear	Disc/drum
General	
Wheelbase, in.	117
Height, in.	53.2
Width, in.	76.6
Length, in.	208
Weight, lb.	4,035
Performance	
0-60 mph	4.8
¼-mile e.t.@mph	13.5@105
Source	*Car and Driver*, 11/1967

it is worthwhile to update with tires, shocks, sway bars and the like because you will probably have to replace everything on the unrestored, abused Road Runner or GTX that is commonly available. Fortunately, because the Road Runner was produced in relatively great numbers, you can still get one at a decent price.

1966-74 Dodge Chargers

Although Dodge products had been doing fairly well on the track, it was obvious that if

For 1969, the Charger SE package was available on the base and R/T. It consisted primarily of a leather interior and complementary trim. *Chrysler Corporation*

A 1969 Charger 500. Aerodynamic aids included flush grille, windshield deflectors and fastback rear window. The Charger 500 grille emblem is missing from this example. *Bud Pennington*

Dodge was to appeal to the ever-increasing youth market, it needed to do more than win races. Dodge had a conservative, blue collar image that just didn't appeal to young people. In 1964 Dodge introduced a "youthfully styled Charger" show car that had some interesting features, but more exciting was the 1965 Charger II show car that greatly resembled the 1966 production version. The Charger II, coupled with a clever advertising

The 1969 Charger Daytona was unstoppable on the NASCAR circuit. Special nose cone, rear wing, flush rear window and other aerodynamic aids made this possible. It's the ultimate Dodge Charger.

campaign—"The Dodge Rebellion wants you!"—managed to increase sales and change Dodge's image.

The centerpiece of Dodge's efforts was the 1966 Charger, which was based on the Coronet body shell but with a fastback roofline. The front grille was similar, but the headlights were retractable, giving the car a more sporty look.

The Charger came with a 318 two-barrel standard, while a 361 two-barrel and 383 four-barrel were optional. The 318 came with a three-speed manual while the larger V-8s got either a four-speed manual or three-speed automatic. A midyear introduction was the 426 Hemi.

The Charger enjoyed modest success with 37,344 sold, but only 468 were built with the 426 Hemi. It did fairly well on the NASCAR circuit, winning the Manufacturers Championship.

The 1967 version was essentially the same except for minor trim changes. The 361 was replaced with a two-barrel version of the 383, and the 440 Magnum rated at 375 hp joined the option list. The 426 Hemi was still available, but only 118 were produced. With sales down to less than 15,000 units, it was obvious that the fastback Charger was not a big hit in the marketplace.

Chrysler's success on the track, however, was to have a significant effect on styling. The 1966–67 Chargers, successful as they were, just did not look that hot on the street. The 1968 Charger did. Totally restyled, the Charger was by far Chrysler's best-looking car in 1968 and its best-looking performance car of the sixties. Whereas Chrysler's other muscle cars provided excellent performance, the Charger provided the same performance but with looks to match. It was a smooth, flowing design.

Model line-up expanded to include the Charger R/T, equipped much like the Coronet R/T. Standard engine was the 440 Magnum rated at 375 hp with the 426 Hemi

For 1970, the Charger got a loop front grille and new rear taillights. The R/T also got a reverse scoop on the front doors.

1971 Dodge Charger SE	
Engine	
Type	V-8
Bore x stroke, in.	4.31 x 3.75
Displacement, cubic in.	440
Compression ratio	9.7:1
Horsepower	305@4600 net
Torque	400@3200 net
Chassis and drivetrain	
Transmission	3-spd automatic
Front suspension	Independent, torsion bars
Rear suspension	Live axle, leaf springs
Axle ratio	3.23:1
Brakes, front/rear	Disc/drum
General	
Wheelbase, in.	115
Height, in.	52.2
Width, in.	79.1
Length, in.	205.4
Weight, lb.	4,092
Performance	
0–60 mph	6.5
¼-mile e.t.@mph	14.8@95.7
Source	*Car and Driver*, 3/1971

optional. Standard equipment included the familiar heavy-duty suspension, brakes and three-speed TorqueFlite automatic while the four-speed manual was optional. The rear

bumblebee stripes were standard but could be deleted.

The base Charger was available with the 225 Slant Six or 318 V-8 as standard equipment with a two-barrel or four-barrel 383 optional.

The Charger was a success on the street, racking up over 90,000 sales, but it was not as competitive on the NASCAR circuit because of aerodynamics. The recessed grille and rear window caused excessive turbulence. By simply substituting a Coronet grille and installing a custom-made rear window over the tunnel backlight, Chrysler made the Charger competitive again. For a car to qualify as a production car, NASCAR rules stated that at least 500 units had to be built; Creative Industries built them. This homologated car was dubbed the Charger 500 due to the 500 production models built.

All Charger 500s were equipped with the 426 Hemi with either the TorqueFlite automatic or four-speed manual transmission and came with all the regular production Hemi mandatory options. The Charger 500 was a 1969 model, and the first competition

This is what a Daytona convertible might have looked like if Dodge ever built one. It's difficult to put a value on a car like this, though it certainly is interesting.

versions saw racing action in early 1969. Unfortunately, it proved to be only competitive rather than an overwhelming winner because Ford brought out special aerodynamic versions of their intermediates, the Torino Talladega and Cyclone Spoiler.

The 1969 production Charger received redesigned taillights while the grille got a divider. Engines and options remained basically the same, but an SE package was available on both the base and Charger R/T. This was a luxury package that included leather front seats and lots of simulated wood on the dash and steering wheel.

The wildest and most famous Charger was the Daytona. It was an all-out attempt to attain supremacy on the NASCAR tracks. The final product of extensive wind-tunnel testing, the car had no equals on the track, and nothing came close to it in terms of visual impact on the street. You immediately noticed the eighteen-inch-long nose cone and high-mounted rear wing, yet other features distinguished it from production

Super Bee model made a brief appearance on the 1971 Charger line.

Chargers as well. The rear window treatment was the same as on the Charger 500s, and the front fenders had reverse-facing scoops—necessary on the race versions for

A 1971 Charger. Front spoiler was optional.

tire clearance. The windshield pillars also had special air deflectors. The Daytona was available with either the 440 Magnum or the 426 Hemi, of which seventy were built. Total production was 503 units, considerably less than the similar looking Super Bird.

With the addition of the Charger 500 and Daytona, 1969 proved to be the high point for the Charger. The 1970 Charger, still based on the same body shell, received a revised loop bumper that did not detract from its good looks. The R/T got simulated scoops on the doors, and instead of the bumblebee stripe, the car got a longitudinal stripe. The car looked better without any stripes, however. The 440 Six Pack was made available on the Charger R/T, but like the Hemi (232 made), it did not prove popular, and Chrysler built only 116.

The model line-up in 1970 included a Charger 500, but it is not to be confused with the 1969 500. This 500 was a specially dressed up base model with the 318 as standard equipment. The SE package was again available but only on the redesigned (now optional) bucket seats. Interestingly, unlike other Chrysler intermediates, the Charger was not available in 1970 with fifteen-inch wheels that would have improved handling.

The 1968–70 Chargers were a hard act to follow, and although the restyled 1971–74 Chargers were attractive automobiles, they lacked the one-two punch of their predecessors. I've always felt that the restyled grille had a Pontiac look to it and that the high beltline made the cars look bigger and heavier even though their wheelbase was two inches shorter and overall length was decreased by three inches.

There were six Charger models for 1971: the base Charger, the Charger hardtop,

From 1972, Dodge put more emphasis on luxury. This is the 1972 Dodge Charger SE. *Chrysler Corporation*

Charger 500, Charger SE, and more interesting, the Charger Super Bee and Charger R/T.

The Charger Super Bee became Dodge's low-buck street racer, replacing the Coronet-based Super Bee of 1970. Standard engine was a 300 hp 383 with a floor-mounted three-speed manual. Optional were the 440 Six Pack and 426 Hemi.

Standard features included Rallye suspension, heavy-duty drum brakes, F70x14 tires, a large Super Bee decal on the blacked-out power bulge of the Ramcharger hood and a cowl-to-side tape stripe treatment. For the drag racer, the Super Trak Pak Performance Axle Package and fifteen-inch Rallye wheels with 60 series tires were available.

Top-of-the-line was the Charger R/T with its standard 440 Magnum rated at 370 hp. Optional were the 440 Six Pack and 426 Hemi. The R/T used the same hood and tape stripe treatment as the Super Bee did, but two additional stripes on each door simulated vents.

Like the rest of Chrysler's performance offerings, 1971 proved to be the last year for the true high-performance Charger. From 1972 to 1974, the performance model was called the Charger Rallye, which was available with increasingly detuned 440 engines.

Prospects

Although the 1966–67 Chargers are interesting cars, and are one of the more successful full fastback designs, they do not quite have the same appeal as the 1968–70s.

The 1968–70 Chargers are classics and favorites among collectors. The styling has held up and even improved with age. It was one of those designs that stood out and because of its uniqueness was not easily copied by other manufacturers. In terms of desirability, the R/T is the obvious favorite, but the base models are also enjoying excellent appreciation. It's going to be tough to

The 1971-74 Chargers may not be as collectible as the earlier versions, but they do have a loyal following.

find an unmodified, unrestored Charger, and as always, try to get one that at least has all the original pieces.

The 1971–74 Chargers lack the performance image of earlier Chargers, which explains their lower prices. Still collectibles of some stature are the 1971 models because they were built with all the right engines, but 440 Six Pack and 426 Hemi production was extremely low, less than 400 units.

Last of the line is the 1974. Even though performance had taken the back seat to luxury, the big 440 was still available. *Chrysler Corporation*

Chapter 8

|---|---|
★★	**1964-69 Barracuda**
★★★	**1964-69 Convertible**
★★	**1970-74 Barracuda**
★★★	**With big-blocks**
★★★★	**With 440 Six Pack**
★★★★★	**With Hemi**
★★★★	**1970-71 Convertible**

1964–74 Plymouth Barracuda

The Barracuda represented Chrysler's entry in the pony car market. From a marketing point of view, it was never much of a contender, never achieving the acceptance and market penetration that the Mustang, Camaro or Firebird had. It seemed that Chrysler kept hedging, waiting until 1970 to make a full commitment with a brand new car. Yet, in retrospect, 1970 was too late because by then the market was in decline. Unfortunately, again, Chrysler stopped production too early. After 1974 the pony car market saw a resurgence with only GM's Camaro and Firebird to take advantage of it.

The pony car had its roots in the Chevrolet Corvair introduced by GM in 1960. Designed to appeal to youthful buyers, the Corvair showed that in an industry where car size was equated with profitability (bigger car equaled bigger profits), a loaded-up compact, correctly marketed, could indeed be profitable. Ford rebodied the Falcon, a successful economy compact, called it the Mustang and watched sales soar.

1964-69

Chrysler took a more cautious approach. Still reeling after the styling excesses of the Exner era, management concentrated on improving the styling of the larger cars

through the efforts of chief stylist Elwood Engel, hired from Ford in 1961. For cost reasons, the Barracuda was based on the Valiant. The most noticeable difference was the unique fastback roof and large rear window. This resulted in a large storage area behind the rear seat, made even larger when the seat was folded over. The rest of the interior was strictly Valiant. A 101 hp 170 ci Slant Six was standard equipment, while a 225 ci Slant Six rated at 145 hp and a two-barrel 273 ci V-8 were optional. A three-speed manual transmission was standard with a four-speed manual and three-speed Torque-Flite automatic optional. Even with the V-8, the Barracuda was not much of a performer, but it was a handsome car.

The 1965 Barracuda was essentially the same car, but the addition of several perfor-

A 1964 Barracuda. *Chrysler Corporation*

1965 Plymouth Barracuda	
Engine	
Type	V-8
Bore x stroke, in.	3.63 x 3.31
Displacement, cubic in.	273
Compression ratio	10.5:1
Horsepower	235@5200
Torque	280@4000
Chassis and drivetrain	
Transmission	4-spd manual
Front suspension	Independent, torsion bars
Rear suspension	Live axle, leaf springs
Axle ratio	3.55:1
Brakes, front/rear	Drum/drum
General	
Wheelbase, in.	106
Height, in.	53.5
Width, in.	70.1
Length, in.	188.2
Weight, lb.	3,170
Performance	
0–60 mph	8.0
¼-mile e.t.@mph	16.1@87
Source	*Motor Trend*, 1/1965

1969 'Cuda 340	
Engine	
Type	V-8
Bore x stroke, in.	4.04 x 3.31
Displacement, cubic in.	340
Compression ratio	10.5:1
Horsepower	275@5000
Torque	340@3200
Chassis and drivetrain	
Transmission	4-spd manual
Front suspension	Independent, torsion bars
Rear suspension	Live axle, leaf springs
Axle ratio	3.91:1
Brakes, front/rear	Disc/drum
General	
Wheelbase, in.	108
Height, in.	52.7
Width, in.	69.6
Length, in.	192.8
Weight, lb.	3,470
Performance	
0–60 mph	7.1
¼-mile e.t.@mph	14.93@96.63
Source	*Car Life*, 11/1968

mance options helped to give the car more of a performance image. The Rallye Pack suspension included heavy-duty shocks and springs, and a front sway bar, while a Commando four-barrel 273 ci V-8 rated at a more respectable 235 hp provided better acceleration. The most distinctive offering in 1965 was the Formula S package which included

The 1965 Barracuda was almost identical to the 1964.

the 235 hp engine, the Rallye Pack suspension and Goodyear Blue Streak tires. Even with the 235 hp V-8, the car could have benefited from more power. You wonder why Chrysler did not offer dual exhausts with this engine.

The Barracuda saw a slight facelift in 1966, but with the exception of a disc brake option, Chrysler made no changes in the performance department. The automotive press found the Barracuda to be a balanced automobile, exhibiting decent handling with adequate power. It was a good, solid car but didn't have the pizzaz the Mustang had to become a success in the marketplace.

In 1967 we saw the first major restyle of the Barracuda. In addition to the fastback, a convertible and a hardtop were available. The fastback and convertible had likable styling, but the hardtop took some getting used to. Engine choice expanded to include a 383 four-barrel V-8 rated at a low 280 hp. Because the engine was such a tight fit, it necessitated the use of restrictive exhaust manifolds, thereby limiting output. And, unfortunately, power steering, power brakes and air conditioning were not available with the big 383, again due to space limitations, making the car a bear to drive. Only 1,841 Formula S 383 Barracudas were built.

The 1968 benefited from some detail changes. The 273 engine was replaced with a 318 rated at 230 hp, while the base engine for the Formula S was a 275 hp 340. The big, heavy 383 was still available, now rated at 300 hp thanks to revised intake manifolding and cylinder heads. For the racetrack, Chrysler built the Barracuda S/S in a limited run of seventy cars, all powered by the 426 Hemi.

If you are interested in 1967–69 Barracudas, forget the big-blocks and get a 340 four-speed. The 340 is a good, strong performer

The 273 ci V-8 provided better performance than the standard six. Emblem on front fenders denoted V-8.

Dash was restyled on the 1965. Shift lever on the column replaced dash-mounted push buttons.

that doesn't ruin the car's inherent good balance. The big engines, which include the limited 440 V-8 of 1969, are just not that much fun to drive, except in a straight line.

The 1969 Barracuda was a carryover with a new grille. The engine line-up remained the same with the 383 now rated at 330 hp. A midyear introduction was the 440 V-8

For 1966, the Barracuda got a slight restyle. This is a Formula S. *Chrysler Corporation*

The 1967–69 Barracudas used the same body
shell. This is a 1969 fastback. The convertible is
particularly attractive.

The 1967–69 hardtop was not as attractive as the other two body styles. It did take some getting used to. *Chrysler Corporation*

rated at 375 hp. *Car Life* did a road test recording a 0–60 mph time of 5.6 seconds and a quarter-mile time of 14.01 at 103.81 mph. The 440, however, was only available with the TorqueFlite automatic, manual drum brakes and manual steering. The 1967–69 Barracudas proved to be disappointments to Chrysler, having been outsold when the figures came in: Barracuda's 139,000 units paled beside Mustang's 1,089,000, Camaro's 605,000 and Firebird's 278,000.

1970-74

The competition was getting tougher. The Mustang in 1969 could be had with the 428 Cobra Jet engine, the Boss 429 Hemi and the high-winding Boss 302. The Camaro could be had with a hairy 396 and a potent 302 Z-28, not to mention the Ram Air 400 Firebird. To be competitive, the Barracuda needed a new body that reflected current styling trends—the long hood and short deck that appealed to the youth market—and needed to accommodate Chrysler's high-performance engines without compromising the car's balance. This, of course, happened with the 1970 model year when the Barracuda underwent a complete restyle based on the new E-body, as was its cousin, the Dodge Challenger.

The 1969 interior. Note sharply bent shifter.

The 1970 'Cuda arrived with a bang, making it a true competitor with other pony cars. This is a Hemi-equipped convertible.

The new body style, available only as a notchback and a convertible, is considered to be the best looking of the three Barracuda generations, and as we shall see, the most desirable as well.

The wheelbase remained the same at 108 inches, but length was reduced six inches, height was reduced two inches and width increased five inches. This made the car look a lot bigger and wider, too wide some said, yet the overall visual effect really depended on what kind of tires the car had. A typical base model with skinny tires did look a bit silly, but the performance models with the 60 series tires looked just right.

Model choices expanded to three: the Barracuda, the performance-oriented 'Cuda and the luxury Gran Coupe. All three were available in either the hardtop or convertible. The 'Cuda, to distinguish it from the plain Barracuda came with a special hood with dual non-functional scoops, hood pins, driving lights, and the rear taillight panel was painted black. Optional was a rear fender "hockey-stick-tape" stripe that indicated engine displacement. The luxury Gran Coupe came with leather bucket seats (vinyl or vinyl and cloth as reduced cost options), an overhead console and distinctive taillight trim.

Of course, what really made the 1970 Barracudas interesting was the engines. A total of nine engines were available if you include the 198 ci Slant Six introduced midyear on the price leader Barracuda Coupe. Base engine on the Barracuda was a 225 ci Slant Six or a 230 hp two-barrel 318. Optional were a two-barrel 383 rated at 275 hp or a four-barrel 383 rated at 330 hp. The Gran Coupe had the same engine availability.

For the performance enthusiasts, the 'Cudas were much more exciting. Standard engine was the four-barrel 383 rated at 335 hp. Optional were the 275 hp 340, 375 hp

The 1970 redesigned interior. This car has the optional Rim Blow steering wheel.

1970 'Cuda

Engine

Type	V-8
Bore x stroke, in.	4.25 x 3.38
Displacement, cubic in.	383
Compression ratio	10.5:1
Horsepower	335@5200
Torque	425@3400

Chassis and drivetrain

Transmission	3-spd automatic
Front suspension	Independent, torsion bars
Rear suspension	Live axle, leaf springs
Axle ratio	3.91:1
Brakes, front/rear	Disc/drum

General

Wheelbase, in.	108
Height, in.	50.9
Width, in.	74.9
Length, in.	186.7
Weight, lb.	3,555

Performance

0–60 mph	NA
¼-mile e.t.@mph	14.40@98.97
Source	*Road Test, 6/1970*

1970 AAR 'Cuda

Engine

Type	V-8
Bore x stroke, in.	4.04 x 3.31
Displacement, cubic in.	340
Compression ratio	10.5:1
Horsepower	290@5000
Torque	345@3400

Chassis and drivetrain

Transmission	4-spd manual
Front suspension	Independent, torsion bars
Rear suspension	Live axle, leaf springs
Axle ratio	3.55:1
Brakes, front/rear	Disc/drum

General

Wheelbase, in.	108
Height, in.	51.9
Width, in.	74.9
Length, in.	186.7
Weight, lb.	3,585

Performance

0–60 mph	5.8
¼-mile e.t.@mph	14.3@99.5
Source	*Car and Driver, 7/1970*

Also optional was the Tuff steering wheel which conveyed more of a performance image to the 'Cuda interior. 'Cudas also came with the optional dash.

four-barrel 440, 390 hp 440 Six Pack and the mighty 425 hp 426 Hemi. With so many different engines, suspension and tire availability can get confusing.

All 'Cudas came with heavy-duty suspensions. The 340 and 383 equipped versions came with heavy-duty torsion bars, springs and shocks with front and rear stabilizer bars, 0.94 inch front, 0.75 inch rear. The big 440 and Hemi came with even heavier front torsion bars and unique rear leaf springs; five leaves with two half-leaves on the left side and six full leaves on the right side with no rear stabilizer bar. This resulted in a rather firm ride that was necessary if you wanted to get all that torque to the ground. The 440 and 426 engines came with a heavy-duty Dana 60 rear axle while the 340s and 383s came with the Chrysler-built 8¾ inch rear in a variety of axle ratios.

Standard brakes were drums, not really recommended for performance use. The optional power front discs provided better stopping power. Transmission choice varied. A three-speed manual was standard

You can identify a 1970 Hemi 'Cuda in two ways: by the hockey-stick rear fender stripes and by the standard shaker hood scoop.

with the 340 and 383 engines, with a four-speed manual or TorqueFlite automatic optional. The 440 and 426 engines came with a specially modified TorqueFlite automatic as standard equipment, with a four-speed manual optional.

On the 'Cuda, F70x14 tires were standard on the Magnum five-spoke rims with the 383 or 440 engines. The 340 powered 'Cuda came with 15x7 inch Rally wheels shod with E60x15 Goodyear Polyglas GTs. The Rally wheels were also optional on the 383 and 440 equipped 'Cudas. On the Hemi 'Cudas, F60x15 tires on the 15x7 Rally wheels were standard. The fourteen-inch Rally wheel was optional as well on the 383s and 440s.

Interesting options, some of which were introduced as the model year progressed, included the elastomeric color-keyed bumpers. These were unchromed bumpers coated with a painted urethane skin matching the car's paint, available in two forms. The first option had just the front bumper and racing mirrors painted; the second option was for

Largest tires available were Goodyear F60x15s.

cars painted in Rallye Red, which could have both front and rear bumpers painted red with matching racing mirrors. The big shaker hood scoop, standard on the Hemi, was optional on the other 'Cudas as well. Rear

The 440 powered 'Cudas were similarly identified. This one has the optional rear wing.

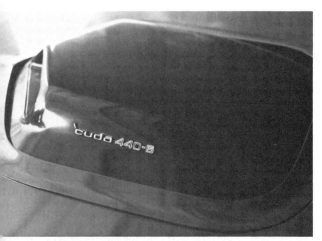

The 440 Six Pack 'Cudas were so designated on the shaker hood.

'Cuda. Two types of rear deck spoilers were available. One had swept-back sides while the other spoiler resembled the unit available on Boss 302 Mustangs. In fact, it was identical to the Ford unit because Chrysler purchased it from the same vendor.

The 1970 model year reached its zenith with the introduction of the AAR 'Cuda, which coincided with Plymouth's entry in the popular Trans-Am race series. To qualify, at least 2,500 street versions of the car had to be built. While Don Gurney's All American Racers built the full race versions, Creative Industries built the unique fiberglass hood and rear spoiler.

The heart of the AAR 'Cuda was a specially modified 340 V-8. It used three two-barrel Holley carburetors mounted on an aluminum Edelbrock intake manifold, special cylinder heads, a solid lifter cam and a reinforced 340 block. It was rated at 290 hp, just like the Boss 302 and Z-28, and provided excellent performance. *Car and Driver* found it could go from 0-60 mph in just 5.8

window louvers, front chin spoilers, hood-mounted tach, Rim Blow steering wheel, Tuff sport steering wheel and a rear deck spoiler were all available to dress up the

Limited-production AAR 'Cuda provided big-block acceleration with handling to match.

146

seconds, and the quarter-mile came in at 14.3 seconds at 99.5 mph.

The rest of the AAR 'Cuda included heavy-duty suspension with a rear sway bar, front discs and rear drum brakes, quick-ratio steering, a side exhaust system and wild side "strobe stripes." The 'Cuda was the only car (besides the Challenger T/A) that came with two different tires, G60x15s on the rear and E60x15s on the front. A four-speed manual or TorqueFlite automatic were the only two transmissions available.

Lacking sufficient development time, the AAR 'Cuda was not successful on the track; however, it was very successful on the street.

In 1971 Chrysler restyled the Barracuda's grille with quad headlights and revised the taillights. Other changes included simulated louvers on the front fenders of the 'Cuda, and along with the color-keyed elastomeric bumpers came a color-keyed grille. Rear side graphics indicating engine displacement replaced the hockey-stick stripes of 1970. In the interior, a split bench seat was optional on the Barracuda and 'Cuda. Leather buckets were still standard on the Gran Coupe and now were optional on the 'Cuda.

Mechanically, the four-barrel 440 was dropped, but otherwise engine selection remained the same. Horsepower ratings were lower, as the industry adopted more realistic net horsepower ratings.

Underrated at 290 hp, the 340 six-barrel was the
only engine available on the AAR 'Cuda.

The year 1972 represented a complete withdrawal from the performance market. All the big engines were dropped. No more shaker hoods, elastomeric bumpers, rear louvers—and no more convertibles. The Barracuda was also scheduled for a major restyle, but unfortunately, sales were just not strong enough to justify the tooling

Major change on the 1971 Barracuda and 'Cuda was this quad headlight cheese-grater grille.

Other changes on the 'Cuda included front fender air extractors and the large rear quarter panel blackout treatment. Window louvers and spoiler were optional.

investment, so the 1972s reverted to a modified single headlight grille, similar to the 1970s', but with a center divider. Model choices were just two: the Barracuda and the 'Cuda. Standard engines were the 225 Slant Six or a two-barrel 318 V-8. Optional on the Barracuda and standard on the 'Cuda was a 240 hp 340. No other engines were available. The 'Cuda got side stripes, and for that performance look, you could get a blacked-out hood treatment.

The years 1973 and 1974 weren't that much different. The six-cylinder engine was dropped, and for the limited-run 1974 model, the 340 engine was replaced with a 360 that was easier to certify for emission standards.

Prospects

From a collector's point of view, the 1970 and 1971 models are the best ones to get.

Not many Hemi or 440 six-barrel 'Cudas were built, and these are commanding high prices, with, naturally, the Hemi-powered cars taking the lead. Expect continued and rapid appreciation here. The same applies to the convertibles and the AAR 'Cudas.

Appreciation is much more modest with the many 383 and 440 four-barrel cars, yet there are some distinct advantages to owning one. That they are much less expensive is obvious, but as important is that they perform almost as well. Their acceleration times are only marginally slower.

As a car appreciates, any modifications to it are frowned upon because strict originality is of paramount importance, especially if you are mainly interested in showing the car. However, with the more plentiful 383s and 440 four-barrel cars, typical bolt-on modifications (which are for the most part

The 1972–74 grille reverted to single headlight configuration. Standard 'Cuda hood scoop had engine size emblems on each side.

easily reversible) will enable enthusiasts to update their cars for better performance without decreasing value. Be aware that the restoration process on a Barracuda can be more difficult than on other pony cars. There is no big reproduction industry making hard-to-find parts for Barracudas simply because production was low. You can almost build a Camaro or Mustang from reproduced parts today. Although more challenging, restoring a Barracuda can be more rewarding.

A 1974 Barracuda with side body tape stripe.
Bob Gilles

★★	1970-71 Challenger
★★★	1970-71 Challenger convertible
★★	1970-71 Challenger SE
★★★★	1970-71 Challenger SE convertible
★★★	1970-71 Challenger R/T, RT/SE
★★★★	1970-71 Challenger R/T, RT/SE convertibles
★★★★	With 440 Six Pack
★★★★★	With Hemi
★★★★	1970 Challenger T/A
★★	1972-74 Challenger and Rallye

1970–74 Dodge Challenger

The Challenger was Dodge's entry in the pony car market. Introduced at the same time as the restyled Plymouth Barracuda of 1970, at first glance, the Challenger looked as though it shared many body parts. However, the only common part was the window glass. The Challenger was built on a longer 110 inch wheelbase and featured a promi-

For 1970, the Dodge Challenger was the equivalent to Plymouth's Barracuda. Styling, at least on the front grille, was more conventional, which probably contributed to the Challenger's greater sales.

nent S-bend side crease. Unlike the Barracuda, the Challenger used quad headlights, while the grille was vaguely reminiscent of those on the 1969 Camaro and 1969–70 Shelby Mustangs. It was, indeed, a handsome car, and although styling is subjective, the public seemed to prefer the Challenger to the Barracuda. The Challenger outsold the Barracuda by a significant margin from 1970 through 1974.

1970-74

Model line-up and engine availability were similar to offerings for the Barracuda. The base model was the Challenger, available as a hardtop or convertible, with either the 225 ci Slant Six or 230 hp two-barrel 318 V-8 as standard equipment. Optional engines were the 275 hp 340, 290 hp 383 and 330 hp 383. A three-speed manual was standard on all these engines, with the exception of the 290

The performance version was the Challenger R/T. *Chrysler Corporation*

hp 383 that came only with the three-speed TorqueFlite automatic. A four-speed manual and three-speed automatic were op-

The Challenger used a full-length rear taillight. This car has optional (probably owner-installed) rear spoiler.

Complementing the AAR 'Cuda was the Dodge Challenger T/A. This particular version, *Western Special,* was available on the West Coast and uses a rear-exit exhaust system.

tional. The same engine line-up was available on the SE. The Challenger SE was similar to the Barracuda Gran Coupe, except that the SE had a smaller rear window.

For the performance enthusiast, Chrysler offered the Challenger R/T. Like the 'Cuda, it came with a performance hood, heavy-duty suspension, Rallye instrument cluster and a choice of longitudinal or bumblebee stripes. Engine availability, suspensions and wheel variations were identical with those for the 'Cuda. However, you could order the SE package on the R/T, which consisted of the formal roof, vinyl roof covering, overhead console, and genuine leather and vinyl bucket seats.

The Dodge equivalent to the AAR 'Cuda was the Challenger T/A. Specifications were identical, although the Challenger used a different hood, which also cropped up on

1970 Dodge Challenger R/T

Engine

Type	V-8
Bore x stroke, in.	4.25 x 3.75
Displacement, cubic in.	426
Compression ratio	10.3:1
Horsepower	425@5000
Torque	490@4000

Chassis and drivetrain

Transmission	3-spd automatic
Front suspension	Independent, torsion bars
Rear suspension	Live axle, leaf springs
Axle ratio	3.23:1
Brakes, front/rear	Drum/drum

General

Wheelbase, in.	110
Height, in.	51.4
Width, in.	76.4
Length, in.	191.3
Weight, lb.	3,890

Performance

0-60 mph	5.8
¼-mile e.t.@mph	14.1@103.2
Source	*Car and Driver*, 11/1969

More common is the side-exhaust system.

some R/Ts. Lacking enough development, the Challenger was not much of a challenge in the 1970 SCCA Trans-Am series, managing a distant fourth. On the street, it was a different matter. The Challenger T/A could easily hold its own against the Boss 302, Camaro Z-28 and the Firebird Trans Am which needed an engine that displaced seventy cubic inches more than the Challenger!

Another midyear entry was the Challenger Deputy which could be had with the small 198 ci version of Chrysler's Slant Six. The rear quarter windows were fixed, but the Deputy was also available with the 225 ci six and the two-barrel and four-barrel 383s.

For the collector and enthusiast, the big-engined Challengers are of interest. Production of the 440 Six Pack was relatively high, with a total of 2,035, ninety-nine of which were R/T convertibles. Hemi production was much less, 356 units, with only nine convertibles.

For 1971, the Challenger was restyled—or at least the grille was. The split grille insert was painted silver, except on the R/T models which were painted black. Other changes for the R/T included color-keyed bumpers, simulated brake cooling scoops in front of the rear wheels and a new side tape treatment. The SE package was not available on the R/T, and the convertible was now available only on the base Challenger.

Engine line-up remained the same for the Challenger R/T; however, as with the rest of the industry, power ratings were revised to reflect net horsepower rather than the previous gross ratings. Thus, for example, the 425 hp Hemi was now rated at 350 hp. No matter how the Hemi was rated, it still provided incredible performance.

Hemi production was low, just seventy-one units. Also, only 250 440 six-barrel Challengers were built. The possibility of obtaining one of these cheaply from some-

For 1971, the grille was restyled on the Challenger.

one who knows what they are has passed, but you never know what you'll be able to find if you look hard enough.

From 1972 on, as with the rest of Chrysler's offerings, Challenger performance was downplayed. The Challenger line-up changed—no more convertibles—with two models offered: the base Challenger and the Rallye. The name Rallye has never evoked images of thundering performance. Equipped with the 240 hp 340 engine, the Rallye's performance was OK with 0-60 mph times in the mid-eight-second range, and you could probably get quarter-mile times down to the low-sixteen range with the optional 3.55 rear axle ratio. The Rallye model came equipped with the performance hood, dual exhausts, simulated air extractors on the front fenders, heavy-duty suspension with front and rear stabilizer bars, front disc brakes and a three-speed manual transmission. A four-speed and TorqueFlite automatic were optional.

Still, it was a handsome car. The grille starting in 1972 was restyled and remained the same until the Challenger's demise in 1974. Engine availability remained the same for 1973, but the Rallye became an optional package on the base Challenger. Standard engine was the 318 with the 340 optional. During the abbreviated 1974 model run, the 360 V-8 replaced the 340 as the top engine.

Prospects

The Challenger was a good car. The 1970-71 models are the ones to get, offering great performance and desirability. The Six Pack and Hemi cars may be getting out of reach, but the plentiful 383 and 440 four-barrel Challengers are still out there at reasonable prices. Many of these will be modified, but as long as these modifications are largely reversible, it shouldn't hurt the value of the car, provided that you are able to return the car to stock with all the correct pieces. This is important because the market for a stock-type car is larger than for a highly modified drag-type car.

As with the Barracuda, parts availability for Challengers is not good. Some body and interior parts are difficult to locate, but engine and driveline parts are plentiful, as they are largely interchangeable with the B-body cars. And you can probably expect that the big-engined Challengers were driven hard and abused.

The 1972–74 Challengers got restyled grilles and taillights.

Chapter 10

Other possibilities for collectors

Taken as a group, 1946–54 Chrysler convertibles, whether they are Chrysler, Dodge, DeSoto or Plymouth, are a pretty good bet because most are in the four-star category.

The 1955–59 convertibles are another group that is appreciating rapidly. All the elements of the Forward Look are evident here, although excessive trim and two- and

The 1956 Chrysler New Yorker convertible is a definite knockout, embodying all elements of Exner's Forward Look. *Don Rook*

three-tone paint may make some of these look a bit garish when compared to a 300 Letter convertible.

Between 1956 and 1961, Dodge did not have an image car to combat Plymouth's Fury, Chrysler's 300 or DeSoto's Adventurer. All Dodges were available with the D-500 option package that consisted of heavy-duty suspension and the highest horsepower optional engine. These Dodges are rare but at the same time, not well known.

The 1967–69 Dodge Dart GT and GTS are at best minor collectibles. Styling was conservative, but with the small-block 340, they do provide excellent performance. Convertibles are rare, as are 383 and 440 powered Darts.

The same applies to the Plymouth Duster and Dodge Demon twins powered with the 340 engine. Built in large numbers, the Duster had a reputation of reliability, and with the 340, it was fast.

It is hard to tell what will be considered a collectible from 1975 on. I think the Dodge Magnum XE and GT produced during 1978 and 1979 are the toughest looking of all the Cordoba derivatives and are good possibilities. Otherwise, besides the 1979 300, nothing really stands out.

The 1957-59 New Yorker convertibles are also a good bet. This is a 1958. *Ron Wenger*

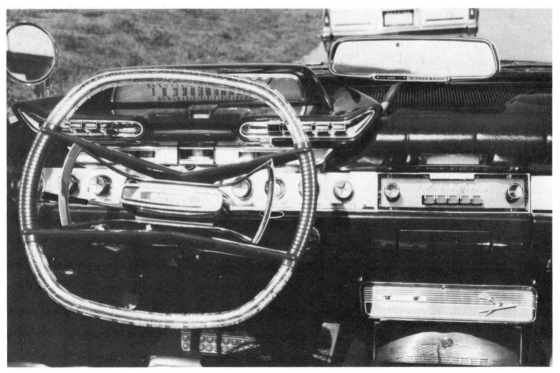

Dodges from 1956 to 1961 equipped with the D-500 option package have more potential than other Dodges. This is a rare 1961 Dodge Polara D-500. Note the funky dash. *Paul Garlich*

The 1968-69 Dodge Dart GT/GTS qualifies as a minor collectible. Shown is the 1969 Dodge Swinger 340. Rare 440 powered cars are a bear to drive. *Chrysler Corporation*

Dodge Demon and Plymouth Duster 340 provide a lot of performance for a small investment. Demon 340, essentially the same as the Duster, is usually less expensive to obtain.

Production figures

Production of Chrysler 300 Letter cars

Model year	Series	Hardtops		Convertibles		Total
		U.S.	Exp.	U.S.	Exp.	
1955	C300	1,692	33*	—	—	1,725
1956	300B	1,060	42*	—	—	1,102
1957	300C	1,737	31	479	5	2,252
1958	300D	588	30	187	4	809
1959	300E	534	16	131	9	690
1960	300F	936	28	240	8	1,212
1961	300G	1,266	14	326	11	1,617
1962	300H	435	—	123	—	558
1963	300J	400	—	—	—	400
1964	300K	3,022	—	625	—	3,647
1965	300L	2,373	32	432	8	2,845

Includes one chassis only.
Source: Chrysler Corporation.

Production of Chrysler non-Letter 300 cars

1962

2dr hdtp	11,341
4dr hdtp	10,030
4dr sedan	1,801
convertible	1,848
Total	25,020

*Includes 306 Pace-
setter Indy 500
Replicas.*

1963

2dr hdtp	9,729*
4dr hdtp	9,915
4dr sedan	1,625
convertible	3,396**
Total	24,665

**Includes 1,861
Pacesetter Indy 500
Replicas.*

Production of Chrysler non-Letter 300 cars

1964

2dr hdtp	10,379*
4dr hdtp	11,460
4dr sedan	2,078
convertible	1,401
Total	28,340

*Includes 255 300
Silver models.*

1965

2dr hdtp	11,621
4dr hdtp	12,452
4dr sedan	2,187
convertible	1,418
Total	27,678

Production of Chrysler non-Letter 300 cars

1966		1967	
2dr hdtp	24,103	2dr hdtp	11,550
4dr hdtp	20,642	4dr hdtp	8,744
4dr sedan	2,352	convertible	1,594
convertible	2,500	Total	21,888
Total	49,597		

1968		1969	
2dr hdtp	16,953	2dr hdtp	16,075
4dr hdtp	15,507	4dr hdtp	14,464
convertible	2,161	convertible	1,933
Total	34,621	Total	32,472

1970		1971	
2dr hdtp	10,084	2dr hdtp	7,256
4dr hdtp	9,846	4dr hdtp	6,683
convertible	1,077	Total	13,939
Total	21,007		
Grand total			279,227

Production of Plymouth Barracudas

1964

6 cyl	2,647
8 cyl	20,796
Total	23,443

1965

6 cyl	18,756
8 cyl	41,601
Total	60,168

1966

6 cyl	10,645
8 cyl	25,536
Total	36,181

1967

	6 cyl	8 cyl
2dr hardtop	10,483	16,277
convertible	859	3,144
2dr sport coupe	5,603	22,425
Total	16,945	41,856
Grand total		58,791

1968

	6 cyl	8 cyl
2dr hardtop	7,402	11,155
convertible	551	2,044
2dr sports coupe	3,290	16,055
Grand total		40,497

1969

	6 cyl	8 cyl
2dr hardtop	4,203	7,548
convertible	300	973
2dr sports coupe	2,163	12,205
Grand total		27,392

Production of Plymouth Barracudas

1970

Barracuda		
2dr hardtop	5,668	17,829
convertible	223	1,169
Gran Coupe		
2dr hardtop	210	7,184
convertible	34	518
'Cuda		
2dr hardtop	—	17,242
convertible	—	550
Grand total		50,627

1971

	6 cyl	8 cly
Barracuda		
2dr hardtop	1,555	6,846
convertible	132	721
Gran Coupe		
2dr hardtop	—	1,298
'Cuda		
2dr hardtop	—	5,314
convertible		293
Grand total		16,159

1972

Barracuda		
2dr hardtop	809	8,951
'Cuda	—	6,382
Grand total		16,142

1973

Barracuda	—	9,976
'Cuda	—	9,305
Grand total		19,281

1974

	—	4,989
Grand total		4,989

*The 1970 model year included 2,724 Plymouth AAR 'Cudas.

Production of Dodge Challengers

1970*	6 cyl	8 cyl
Challenger		
2dr hdtp	9,929	39,350
2dr fstbk	350	5,873
convertible	378	2,543
Challenger R/T		
2dr hdtp	—	13,796
2dr fstbk	—	3,753
convertible	—	963
Grand total		76,935

1971	6 cyl	8 cyl
Challenger		
2dr hdtp	1,672	18,956
convertible	83	1,774

Production of Dodge Challengers

1971	6 cyl	8 cyl
Challenger R/T		
2dr hdtp	—	3,814
Grand total		26,299
1972		
Challenger		
2dr hdtp	842	15,175
Challenger Rallye		
2dr hdtp	—	6,902
Grand total		22,919
1973		
Challenger		
2dr hdtp	—	27,930
Grand total		27,930
1974		
Challenger		
2dr hdtp	—	6,063
Grand total		6,063

*The 1970 model year included 2,399 Challenger T/As.

Production of Dodge Chargers

1966	6 cyl	8 cyl
2dr	—	37,344
Grand total		37,344
1967		
2dr	—	14,980
Grand total		14,980
1968		
2dr	906	74,019
2dr R/T	—	17,665
Grand total		92,590
1969*		
2dr	542	65,840
2dr R/T	—	19,298
Grand total		85,680
1970		
2dr	211	9,163
2dr 500	—	27,432
2dr R/T	—	9,509
Grand total		46,315
1971		
2dr	116	355
2dr Custom	1,441	40,123
2dr 500	—	10,306
2dr SE	—	14,641
2dr Super Bee	—	4,144
2dr R/T	—	2,659
Grand total		73,785
1972		
2dr	813	5,557

Production of Dodge Chargers

1972	6 cyl	8 cyl
2dr Custom	132	41,585
2dr SE	—	20,266
Grand total		68,353
1973		
2dr	931	8,857
2dr Custom	374	40,783
2dr SE	—	57,026
Grand total		107,971
1974		
2dr Custom	1,013	23,703
2dr SE	—	30,957
Grand total		55,673

*The 1969 model year included 503 Daytonas and 500 Charger 500s.

Production of Plymouth Belvedere GTXs and Road Runners

Plymouth Belvedere GTX

1967		1968	
2dr hdtp	11,429	2dr hdtp	17,246
convertible	686	convertible	1,026
Total	12,115	Total	18,272
1969		**1970**	
2dr hdtp	14,385	2dr hdtp	7,202
convertible	625	**1971**	
Total	15,010	2dr hdtp	2,626
Grand total			55,225

Plymouth Road Runner

1968		1969	
2dr coupe	29,240	2dr coupe	32,717
2dr hdtp	15,358	2dr hdtp	47,365
Total	44,598	convertible	2,027
		Total	82,109
1970		**1971**	
2dr coupe	14,744	2dr hdtp	13,046
convertible	684	**1972**	
2dr hdtp	20,899	2dr hdtp	6,831
Super Bird	2,783*	**1973**	
Total	39,110	2dr hdtp	17,443
		1974	
		2dr hdtp	9,656
Grand total			212,793

*Other quoted production figures are 1,920, 1,935 and 1,971.

Production of Dodge Coronet R/Ts

1967		1968	
2dr hdtp	9,553	2dr hdtp	9,989
convertible	628	convertible	569
Total	10,181	Total	10,558
1969		**1970**	
2dr hdtp	6,518	2dr hdtp	2,172
convertible	437	convertible	236
Total	6,955	Total	2,408
		Grand total	30,102

Production of Dodge Super Bees

1968		1969	
2dr coupe	7,842	2dr coupe	7,650
		2dr hdtp	18,475
		Total	26,125
1970		**1971**	
2dr coupe	3,640	2dr hdtp	4,144
2dr hdtp	10,614		
Total	14,254		
		Grand total	52,365

Production of Plymouth Fury GTs

1970		1971	
2dr hdtp (PP-23)	666	2dr hdtp (PP-23)	333
2dr hdtp (PS-23)	689		
Total	1,355		
		Grand total	1,688

Production of Plymouth Duster 340s

1970	21,799	1971	10,403
1972	14,132	1973	13,862
Grand total			60,196

Production of Dodge Demon 340s

1971	7,899	1972	8,739
1973	9,880		
Grand total			26,518

Production of Dodge Dart GTSs

1968		1969	
2dr hdtp	7,699	2dr hdtp	5,717
convertible	403	convertible	360
Total	8,102	Total	6,077
		Grand total	14,179

Source: Chrysler Corporation.

Production of DeSoto Pacesetters and Adventurers

Pacesetter

1956

convertible 100–400 (est.)

Adventurer

1956		1957	
2dr hdtp	996	2dr hdtp	1,650
Total	996	convertible	300
		Total	1,950
1958		**1959**	
2dr hdtp	350	2dr hdtp	590
convertible	82	convertible	97
Total	432	Total	687
1960			
2dr hdtp	3,092		
4dr hdtp	1,958		
4dr sedan	9,032		
Total	14,082		

Grand total Adventurer production 18,147

Production of Plymouth Furys

1956-58

1956	
2dr hdtp	4,485
1957	
2dr hdtp	7,438
1958	
2dr hdtp	5,303
1956–58 Total	17,226

1959

Plymouth Fury	
2dr hdtp	21,494
2dr hdtp	13,614
4dr sedan	30,149
Plymouth Sport Fury	
2dr hdtp	17,867
2dr convertible	5,990
1959 Total	89,114

Production of Town & Country cars

Model year Type (cylinders-wheelbase)	Production United States	Export
1941		
Station wagon, 9 pass. (6–121½")	796	3

Production of Town & Country cars

Model year

Type (cylinders-wheelbase)	Production United States	Export
1941		
Station wagon, 6 pass. (6–121½")	200	0
Station wagon, 9 pass. (8–127½")	1	0
Total	997	3
1942		
Station wagon, 9 pass. (6–121½")	849	0
Station wagon, 6 pass. (6–121½")	150	0
Station wagon, 9 pass. (8–127½")	1	0
Total	1,000	0
1946		
Four-door sedan (6–121½")	123	0
Two-door Brougham (6–121½")	1	0
Two-door convertible (6–121½")	1	0
Two-door convertible (8–127½")	2,035	89*
Two-door hardtop coupe (8–127½")	7	0
Total	2,167	89
1947		
Four-door sedan (6–121½")	2,751	0
Two-door convertible (8–127½")	3,136	0*
Total	5,887	0
1948		
Four-door sedan (6–121½")	1,175	0
Two-door convertible (8–127½")	3,309	0*
Total	4,484	0
1949		
Two-door convertible (8–131½")	993	7
1950		
Two-door Newport hardtop (8–131½")	698	2

Combined production for 1946–48.
Source: Compiled by Don Narus.

Production of Imperials

1955
Imperial C-69

4dr sedan	7,840
hardtop	3,418
convertible (special body)	1
chassis	1
Total	11,260
Crown Imperial C-70	
limousine	127
8 p sedan	45
Total	172
1955 Total	11,432

1956
Imperial C-73

4dr sedan	6,821
2dr hardtop	2,094
4dr hardtop	1,543
Total	10,458
Crown Imperial C-70	
limousine	175
8 p sedan	51
Total	226
1956 Total	10,684

1957
Imperial IM1-1

4dr hardtop	7,527
4dr sedan	5,654
2dr hardtop	4,885
Total	18,066
Imperial Crown IM1-2	
4dr hardtop	7,843
2dr hardtop	4,199
4dr sedan	3,642
convertible	1,167
Total	16,851
Imperial LeBaron IM1-4	
4dr sedan	1,729
4dr hardtop	911
Total	2,640
1957 Total	37,557

1958
Imperial LY1-L

4dr hardtop	3,336
4dr sedan	1,926

1958
Imperial LY1-L

2dr hardtop	1,801
Total	7,063

Imperial Crown LY1-M

4dr hardtop	4,146
2dr hardtop	1,939
4dr hardtop	1,240
convertible	675
Total	8,000

Imperial LeBaron LY1-H

4dr hardtop	538
4dr sedan	501
Total	1,039
1958 Total	16,102

1959
Imperial Custom MY1-L

4dr hardtop	3,984
4dr sedan	2,071
2dr hardtop	1,743
Total	7,798

Imperial Crown MY1-M

4dr hardtop	4,714
2dr hardtop	1,728
4dr sedan	1,335
convertible	555
Total	8,332

Imperial LeBaron MY1-H

4dr hardtop	622
4dr sedan	510
Total	1,132
1959 Total	17,262

1960
Imperial Custom PY1-L

4dr hardtop	3,953
4dr sedan	2,335
2dr hardtop	1,498
Total	7,786

Imperial Crown PY1-M

4dr hardtop	4,510
4dr sedan	1,594
2dr hardtop	1,504
convertible	618
Total	8,226

Imperial LeBaron PY1-H

4dr hardtop	999
4dr sedan	692
Total	1,691
1960 Total	17,703

1961
Imperial Custom RY1-L

4dr hardtop	4,129
2dr hardtop	889
Total	5,018

Imperial Crown RY1-M

4dr hardtop	4,769
2dr hardtop	1,007
convertible	429
Total	6,205

Imperial LeBaron RY1-H

4dr hardtop	1,026
1961 Total	12,249

1962
Imperial Custom SY1-L

4dr hardtop	3,587
2dr hardtop	826
Total	4,413

Imperial Crown SY2-M

4dr hardtop	6,911
2dr hardtop	1,010
convertible	554
Total	8,475

Imperial LeBaron

4dr hardtop	1,449
1962 Total	14,337

1963
Imperial Custom TY1-L

4dr hardtop	3,264
2dr hardtop	749
Total	4,013

Imperial Custom TY1-M

4dr hardtop	6,960
2dr hardtop	1,067
convertible	531
Total	8,558

Imperial LeBaron TY1-H

4dr hardtop	1,537
1963 Total	14,108

1964
Imperial Crown VY1-M

4dr hardtop	14,181
2dr hardtop	5,233
convertible	922
Total	20,336

Imperial LeBaron VY1-H

4dr hardtop	2,949
1964 Total	23,285

1965

Imperial Crown AY1-M

4dr hardtop	11,628
2dr hardtop	3,974
convertible	633
Total	16,235

Imperial LeBaron AY1-H

4dr hardtop	2,164
1965 Total	18,399

1966

Imperial Crown BY1-M

4dr hardtop	8,977
2dr hardtop	2,373
convertible	514
Total	11,864

Imperial LeBaron BY1-H

4dr hardtop	1,878
1966 Total	13,742

1967

Imperial Crown CY1-M

4dr hardtop	9,415
2dr hardtop	3,235
4dr sedan	2,193
convertible	577
Total	15,420

Imperial LeBaron CY1-H

4dr hardtop	2,194
1967 Total	17,614

1968

Imperial Crown DY1-M

4dr hardtop	8,492
2dr hardtop	2,656
4dr sedan	1,887
convertible	474
Total	13,509

Imperial LeBaron DY1-H

4dr hardtop	1,852
1968 Total	15,361

1969

Imperial EY-M

4dr hardtop (LeBaron)	14,821
(Crown)	823
2dr hardtop (LeBaron)	4,572
(Crown)	244
4dr sedan (Crown)	1,617
Total	22,077

1970

Imperial Crown FY-L

4dr hardtop	1,333
2dr hardtop	254
Total	1,587

Imperial LeBaron FY-M

4dr hardtop	8,426
2dr hardtop	1,803
Total	10,229
1970 Total	11,816

1971

Imperial LeBaron GY-M

4dr hardtop	10,116
2dr hardtop	1,442
Total	11,558

1972

Imperial LeBaron HY-M

4dr hardtop	13,472
2dr hardtop	2,322
Total	15,794

1973

Imperial LeBaron 3Y-M

4dr hardtop	14,166
2dr hardtop	2,563
Total	16,729

1974

Imperial LeBaron 4Y-M

4dr hardtop	10,576
2dr hardtop	3,850
Total	14,426

1975

Imperial LeBaron 5Y-M

4dr hardtop	6,102
2dr hardtop	2,728
Total	8,830

Source: Chrysler and Imperial: The Postwar Years, *Richard M. Langworth as compiled by Jeffrey I Godshall.*

Production of Ghia Imperials

1957	36	1962	—
1958	31	1963	13
1959	7	1964	10
1960	16	1965	10
1961	9	Total	132

Serial numbers of 1969-72 440 three two-barrels

Location 1969-72: on a plate attached to the left side of instrument panel, visible through windshield.

First digit: Car line
- B = Barracuda
- J = Challenger
- P = Fury
- R = Belvedere/Satellite
- W = Coronet 1969-70
- W = Charger 1971
- X = Charger 1970-71

Second digit: Price class
- H = High
- M = Medium
- P = Premium
- S = Special

Third and fourth digits: Body type
- 21 = 2dr coupe
- 23 = 2dr hardtop
- 27 = convertible
- 29 = 2dr sports hardtop

Fifth digit: Engine
- M = Special-order V-8 engine 1969 A12 pkg
- V = 440 3x2bbl engine

Sixth digit: Model year
- 9 = 1969
- 0 = 1970
- 1 = 1971
- 2 = 1972

Seventh digit: Assembly plant
- A = Lynch Road, MI
- B = Hamtramck, MI
- E = Los Angeles, CA
- F = Newark, DE
- G = St. Louis, MO
- R = Windsor, ONT Canada

Last six digits indicate sequence number.

Production of 1969-72 440 three two-barrels

Vin #	Year	Model	Body style	Total
WM21M9	1969	Super Bee	2dr coupe	1,487
WM23M9	1969	Super Bee	2dr hardtop	420
RM21M9	1969	Road Runner	2dr coupe	615
RM23M9	1969	Road Runner	2dr hardtop	817
JS23V0	1970	Challenger R/T	2dr hardtop	1,640
JS27V0	1970	Challenger R/T	convertible	99
JS29V0	1970	Challenger R/T SE	2dr sports hardtop	296
WM21V0	1970	Super Bee	2dr coupe	196
WM23V0	1970	Super Bee	2dr hardtop	1,072
WS23V0	1970	Coronet R/T	2dr hardtop	194
WS27V0	1970	Coronet R/T	convertible	16
XS29V0	1970	Charger R/T	2dr sports hardtop	116
BS23V0	1970	'Cuda	2dr hardtop	1,755
BS27V0	1970	'Cuda	convertible	29
RM21V0	1970	Road Runner	2dr coupe	651
RM23V0	1970	Road Runner	2dr hardtop	1,846
RM23V0	1970	Super Bird	2dr hardtop	716
RM27V0	1970	Road Runner	convertible	34
RS23V0	1970	GTX	2dr hardtop	678
PP23V0	1970	Sport Fury GT	2dr hardtop	1*
JS23V1	1971	Challenger R/T	2dr hardtop	250
WM23V1	1971	Super Bee	2dr hardtop	99
WS23V1	1971	Charger R/T	2dr hardtop	178
BS23V1	1971	'Cuda	2dr hardtop	237
BS27V1	1971	'Cuda	convertible	17
RM23V1	1971	Road Runner	2dr hardtop	246

Production of 1969–72 440 three two-barrels

Vin #	Year	Model	Body style	Total
RS23V1	1971	GTX	2dr hardtop	135
WH21V2	1972	Charger Rallye	2dr coupe	0*
WH23V2	1972	Charger Rallye	2dr hardtop	2*
RM23V2	1972	Road Runner/GTX	2dr hardtop	1*

When a production total is not known, records show the number known to exist. If proof of production is known, but none are known to exist, records will show 0. Records are for US specifications.
Source: Galen Govier.

Serial numbers of 1966–71 426 Hemi

Location 1966–67 on a plate attached to the left front hinge pillar post.
Location 1968–71 on a plate attached to the left side of instrument panel, visible through windshield.
First digit: Car line
    B = Barracuda
    J = Challenger
    L = Dart
    R = Belvedere/Satellite
    W = Coronet 1969–70
    W = Charger 1971
    X = Charger 1966–70
Second digit: Price class
    E = Economy
    L = Low
    H = High
    M = Medium
    O = Super stock
    P = Premium
    S = Special
    X = Fast top
Third and fourth digits: Body type
    21 = 2dr sedan/coupe
    23 = 2dr hardtop
    27 = convertible
    29 = 2dr sports hardtop
    41 = 4dr sedan
Fifth digit: Engine
    H = 426 2x4bbl Hemi engine stage I mechanical lifters 5qt oil pan 1966
    J = 426 2x4bbl Hemi engine stage I mechanical lifters 5qt oil pan 1967
    J = 426 2x4bbl Hemi engine stage II mechanical lifters 6qt oil pan 1968–69
    R = 426 2x4bbl Hemi engine stage III hydraulic lifters 6qt oil pan 1970–71
    M = Special-order V-8 engine (1968 S/S Hemi)
Sixth digit: Model year
    6 = 1966
    7 = 1967
    8 = 1968
    9 = 1969
    0 = 1970

continued

Serial numbers of 1966–71 426 Hemi continued

Seventh Digit: Assembly plant

1 = Lynch Road, MI 1966–67	A = Lynch Road, MI 1968–71
2 = Hamtramck, MI 1966–67	B = Hamtramck, MI 1968–71
7 = St. Louis, MO 1966–67	G = St. Louis, MO 1968–71
9 = Windsor, ONT Canada 1966–67	R = Windsor, ONT Canada 1968–71

Note: 426 Hemi engine was not installed at Los Angeles assembly plant.

Last six digits indicate sequence number.

Vin #	Year	Model	Body style	Total

Production of 1966–71 426 Hemi

Vin #	Year	Model	Body style	Total
WE21H6	1966	Coronet	2dr sedan	34
WE41H6	1966	Coronet Deluxe	4dr sedan	2*
WL21H6	1966	Coronet Deluxe	2dr sedan	49
WH23H6	1966	Coronet 440	2dr hardtop	288
WH27H6	1966	Coronet 440	convertible	6
WP23H6	1966	Coronet 500	2dr hardtop	340
WP27H6	1966	Coronet 500	convertible	21
XP29H6	1966	Charger	2dr sports hardtop	468
RL21H6	1966	Belvedere I	2dr sedan	136
RH23H6	1966	Belvedere II	2dr hardtop	531
RH27H6	1966	Belvedere II	convertible	10
RH45H6	1966	Belvedere II	6 p wagon	1*
RP23H6	1966	Satellite	2dr hardtop	817
RP27H6	1966	Satellite	convertible	27
WL21J7	1967	Coronet Deluxe	2dr sedan	1*
WO23J7	1967	Coronet 440 S/S	2dr hardtop	55
WP23J7	1967	Coronet 500	2dr hardtop	0*
WS23J7	1967	Coronet R/T	2dr hardtop	
WS27J7	1967	Coronet R/T	convertible	
			Combined total, hardtop and convertible	283
XP29J7	1967	Charger	2dr sports hardtop	118
RH21J7	1967	Belvedere I	2dr sedan	1*
RO23J7	1967	Belvedere II S/S	2dr hardtop	55
RH23J7	1967	Belvedere II	2dr hardtop	3*
RP23J7	1967	Satellite	2dr hardtop	3*
RP27J7	1967	Satellite	convertible	1*
RS23J7	1967	Belvedere GTX	2dr hardtop	
RS27J7	1967	Belvedere GTX	convertible	
			Combined total, hardtop and convertible	720
LO23M8	1968	Dart S/S	2dr hardtop	80
WM21J8	1968	Super Bee	2dr coupe	125
WH21J8	1968	Coronet 440	2dr coupe	2*
WS23J8	1968	Coronet R/T	2dr hardtop	220
WS27J8	1968	Coronet R/T	convertible	9
XS29J8	1968	Charger R/T	2dr sports hardtop [Includes one Charger 500 prototype]	468

Vin #	Year	Model	Body style	Total

Production of 1966–71 426 Hemi

Vin #	Year	Model	Body style	Total

Vin #	Year	Model	Body style	Total
BO29M8	1968	Barracuda S/S	2dr sports hardtop	70
RM21J8	1968	Road Runner	2dr coupe	
RM23J8	1968	Road Runner	2dr hardtop	
			Combined total, coupe and hardtop	1,019
RS23J8	1968	GTX	2dr hardtop	410
RS27J8	1968	GTX	convertible	36
WM21J9	1969	Super Bee	2dr coupe	166
WM23J9	1969	Super Bee	2dr hardtop	92
WS23J9	1969	Coronet R/T	2dr hardtop	97
WS27J9	1969	Coronet R/T	convertible	10
XS29J9	1969	Charger R/T	2dr hardtop	232
XX29J9	1969	Charger 500	2dr fast top	52*
XX29J9	1969	Charger Daytona	2dr fast top	70
RM21J9	1969	Road Runner	2dr coupe	356
RM23J9	1969	Road Runner	2dr hardtop	422
RM27J9	1969	Road Runner	convertible	10
RS23J9	1969	GTX	2dr hardtop	198
RS27J9	1969	GTX	convertible	11
JS23R0	1970	Challenger R/T	2dr hardtop	287
JS27R0	1970	Challenger R/T	convertible	9
JS29R0	1970	Challenger RT/SE	2dr sports hardtop	60
WM21R0	1970	Super Bee	2dr coupe	4
WM23R0	1970	Super Bee	2dr hardtop	32
WS23R0	1970	Coronet R/T	2dr hardtop	13
WS27R0	1970	Coronet R/T	convertible	1*
XS29K0	1970	Charger R/T	2dr sports hardtop	112
BS23R0	1970	Hemi 'Cuda	2dr hardtop	652
BS27R0	1970	Hemi 'Cuda	convertible	14
RM21R0	1970	Road Runner	2dr coupe	74
RM23R0	1970	Road Runner	2dr hardtop	75
RM23R0	1970	Super Bird	2dr hardtop	135
RM27R0	1970	Road Runner	convertible	3
RS23R0	1970	GTX	2dr hardtop	72
JS23R1	1971	Challenger R/T	2dr hardtop	71
WM23R1	1971	Super Bee	2dr hardtop	22
WS23R1	1971	Charger R/T	2dr hardtop	63
BS23R1	1971	Hemi 'Cuda	2dr hardtop	108
BS27R1	1971	Hemi 'Cuda	convertible	7
RM23R1	1971	Road Runner	2dr hardtop	55
RS23R1	1971	GTX	2dr hardtop	30

*When a production total is not known, records show the number known to exist. If proof of production is known, but none are known to exist, records will show 0. Records are for US specifications.

Source: Galen Govier.

Mopar clubs

W.P.C. Club, Inc.
P.O. Box 3504
Kalamazoo, MI 49003
   Founded 1969, the largest Chrysler products club. More than 20 regions, annual summer national meet and international winter photo meet. Publishes *WPC News*, a high-quality monthly publication, featuring all eras of Chrysler products.

MoPar Muscle Club International
Route 9, Box 18
Lockport, IL 60441
   Founded 1978, primarily focuses on 1960s and 1970s high-performance Chrysler cars. Publishes *Muscle Hustle*, an excellent monthly with many interesting features and articles.

Chrysler 300 Club, Inc.
1333 Branchwater Lane
Birmingham, AL 35216
   Founded 1969, covers all Chrysler 300s, Letter and non-Letter. Many chapters and regions, publishes *Brute Force* bimonthly. Many local meets and annual convention.

Chrysler 300 Club International, Inc.
19 Donegal Court
Ann Arbor, MI 48104
   Founded 1969, caters primarily to 300 Letter Series, although ownership is not re-quired. Many chapters and meets through the year.

Imperial Owners Club International
P.O. Box 991
Scranton, PA 18503
   Founded 1976. Publishes *The Imperial Times* bimonthly, covers all Imperials from 1926 to 1983, extensive want-ads and parts location assistance.

DeSoto Club of America
105 E 96th
Kansas City, MO 64114
   Founded 1972, dedicated to preserving and restoring the DeSoto automobile. Publishes newsletter *DeSoto Days*.

National DeSoto Club, Inc.
412 Cumnock Road
Inverness, IL 60067
   Founded 1986, with over 1,000 members. Publishes *DeSoto Adventures* bimonthly. Annual convention and local meets.

Plymouth Barracuda/'Cuda Owners Club
RD4, Box 61
Borthampton, PA 18067
   Founded 1978, devoted to Barracuda/'Cuda. Publishes bimonthly publication. National meet.

National Hemi Owners Association
170 Pansy Pike
Blanchester, OH 45107
Founded 1975, open to owners and enthusiasts of Chrysler Hemi-powered vehicles.

Northeast Hemi Owners Association
P.O. Box 426
St. Peters, PA 19470
Dedicated to preserving, restoring and enjoying Chrysler performance vehicles. Two meets per year in the Northeast. Publishes bimonthly newsletter.

Daytona/Super Bird Automobile Club
13717 Green Meadow
New Berlin, WI 53151
Dedicated to the Daytona and Super Bird.

National Chrysler Products Club
P.O. Box 3150
Falls Church, VA 22043
National club covering all Chrysler cars. Many local chapters and meets.

Chrysler Products Slant Six Club
14 Fairview Place
New Rochelle, NY 10805
Main focus is on Slant Six-powered Mopars. Newsletter and many meets.

The Chrysler Town & Country Owners Registry
406 W. 34th Street
Kansas City, MO 64111
The club for owners and enthusiasts of 1941–50 Chrysler wooden-bodied cars. Quarterly publication.